Student Companion to

Stephen CRANE

Student Companion to
Stephen
Crane

Paul M. Sorrentino

Student Companions to Classic Writers

Greenwood Press
Westport, Connecticut • London

WILLIAMSBURG REGIONAL LIBRARY
7770 CROAKER ROAD
WILLIAMSBURG, VIRGINIA 23188

AUG - - 2008

Library of Congress Cataloging-in-Publication Data

Sorrentino, Paul.
  Student companion to Stephen Crane / Paul M. Sorrentino.
    p. cm.—(Student companions to classic writers, ISSN 1522-7979)
  Includes bibliographical references and index.
  ISBN 0-313-33104-9 (alk. paper)
    1. Crane, Stephen, 1871-1900—Criticism and interpretation—Handbooks,
  manuals, etc. I. Title. II. Series.
  PS1449.C85Z87   2006
  813'.4—dc22   2005026301

British Library Cataloguing in Publication Data is available.

Copyright © 2006 by Paul M. Sorrentino

All rights reserved. No portion of this book may be
reproduced, by any process or technique, without the
express written consent of the publisher.

Library of Congress Catalog Card Number: 2005026301
ISBN: 0-313-33104-9
ISSN: 1522-7979

First published in 2006

Greenwood Press, 88 Post Road West, Westport, CT 06881
An imprint of Greenwood Publishing Group, Inc.
www.greenwood.com

Printed in the United States of America

The paper used in this book complies with the
Permanent Paper Standard issued by the National
Information Standards Organization (Z39.48-1984).

10 9 8 7 6 5 4 3 2 1

Contents

Series Foreword

This series has been designed to meet the needs of students and general readers for accessible literary criticism on the American and world writers most frequently studied and read in the secondary school, community college, and four-year college classrooms. Unlike other works of literary criticism that are written for the specialist and graduate student, or that feature a variety of reprinted scholarly essays on sometimes obscure aspects of the writer's work, the Student Companions to Classic Writers series is carefully crafted to examine each writer's major works fully and in a systematic way, at the level of the nonspecialist and general reader. The objective is to enable the reader to gain a deeper understanding of the work and to apply critical thinking skills to the act of reading. The proven format for the volumes in this series was developed by an advisory board of teachers and librarians for a successful series published by Greenwood Press, Critical Companions to Popular Contemporary Writers. Responding to their request for easy-to-use and yet challenging literary criticism for students and adult library patrons, Greenwood Press developed a systematic format that is not intimidating but helps the reader to develop the ability to analyze literature.

How does this work? Each volume in the Student Companions to Classic Writers series is written by a subject specialist, an academic who understands students' needs for basic and yet challenging examination of the writer's canon. Each volume begins with a biographical chapter, drawn from published sources, biographies, and autobiographies, that relates the writer's life to his or her work. The next chapter examines the writer's literary heritage, tracing the literary influences of other writers on that writer and explaining and discussing the literary genres into which the writer's work falls. Each of the following chapters examines a major work by the writer, those works most frequently read and studied by high school and college students. Depending on the writer's canon, generally between four and eight major works are examined, each in an individual chapter. The discussion of each work is organized into separate sections on plot development, character development, and major themes. Literary devices and style, narrative point of view, and historical setting are also discussed in turn if pertinent to the work. Each chapter concludes with an alternate critical perspective from which to read the work, such as a psychological or feminist criticism. The critical theory is defined briefly in easy, comprehensible language for the student. Looking at the literature from the point of view of a particular critical approach will help the reader to understand and apply critical theory to the act of reading and analyzing literature.

Of particular value in each volume is the bibliography, which includes a complete bibliography of the writer's works, a selected bibliography of biographical and critical works suitable for students, and lists of reviews of each work examined in the companion, both from the time the literature was originally published and from contemporary sources, all of which will be helpful to readers, teachers, and librarians who would like to consult additional sources.

As a source of literary criticism for the student or for the general reader, this series will help the reader to gain understanding of the writer's work and skill in critical reading.

1

The Life of Stephen Crane

CHILDHOOD

Stephen Crane was born on November 1, 1871, in Newark, New Jersey, to the Reverend Dr. Jonathan Townley Crane, a well-known Methodist minister, and Mary Helen Peck Crane, a leader in church activities and the New Jersey Women's Christian Temperance Movement. He was their 14th child, of whom only 8 were alive at the time of his birth. He was named after several previous Stephens, most notably his Revolutionary War namesake (1709–80), who had been president of the Colonial Assemblies and delegate from New Jersey to the Continental Congress in Philadelphia. Crane's father served as a minister in several churches in New Jersey before moving to Port Jervis, New York, in 1878 to become pastor of a local church, a position he held until his unexpected death in 1880.

The influence of Crane's ancestry on him was evident throughout his life. On his father's side, the Crane family was especially proud of its genealogical roots in the colonies, tracing them back to seventeenth-century New England. Crane's Revolutionary War namesake would have signed the Declaration of Independence had he not been called back home in June 1776 to help settle a political crisis involving Tories in the New Jersey legislature; the Crane family—including Stephen himself—mistakenly believed he had been one of the signers. Similarly, his mother's father and his four brothers were prominent ministers. George Peck edited the *Methodist Quarterly Review* and later the *Christian Advocate and Journal* and authored several books that Stephen would later use as a resource for short stories. Rev. Peck's brother Jesse Truesdell Peck was a bishop in the Methodist Episcopal Church. He cofounded Syracuse University, a fact that Stephen's mother drew upon when she encouraged him to enroll there in 1891, and, like his brother George, he was a prolific author on religious and historical matters. Stephen was familiar with his family's publications. Rev. Jesse Peck's *What Must I Do to Be Saved?* (1858) was given to Stephen by his father in 1881, remained in his library until his death in 1900, and had a great influence on his literary and philosophical outlook.

In addition to having a proud lineage, Stephen was born into a family of writers. His father wrote several religious tracts and scores of articles on moral issues, his mother wrote short stories and religious columns for local newspapers, his sister Agnes was an aspiring writer who published short stories, and his brother Jonathan Townley was a journalist. Accounts of Stephen's first years emphasize how literate he was as a child. Before he was two, he was writing letters to his grandmother, telling his father when he wanted "to yite to ganma" (*Log* 6), and spelling and pronouncing words of five and six syllables with the help of his brother Edmund. By the age of three he had taught himself to read (10). Reminiscences recount his fascination with language. Once when asked his name, he created a fictional persona for himself, "nome Pe-pop-ty," which, though unrecognizable to anyone in the family, remained for his sister Nellie an affectionate nickname for him even as an adult. On another occasion, "Stevie" imitated his brother Townley, who would sometimes ask his mother the correct spelling of a word while writing a news story: "Stevie was making weird marks on a paper with a lead pencil one day and in the exact tone of one, absorbed in composition, and coming to the surface only for a moment for needed information, called to his mother, 'Ma, how do you spell "O"?,' this happening to be a letter he had just become acquainted with" (8).

SCHOOLING

Like two of his senior contemporaries in American fiction, Mark Twain and Henry James, Stephen Crane never completed a course of study in any educational institution. Delicate health prevented regular school attendance until he was eight years old. After his father died in 1880, his mother moved the family from Port Jervis to a boarding house in Roseville near Newark and back to Port Jervis for a time when Stephen developed scarlet fever. From Roseville, the Cranes went to Asbury Park on the New Jersey shore, where Stephen presumably attended school from 1883 until fall 1885, when he entered Pennington Seminary, a coeducational Methodist boarding school in Pennington, New Jersey, of which his father had been principal from 1849 to 1858. Before graduating, he transferred to Claverack College and Hudson River Institute, a coeducational, semimilitary high school and junior college in Columbia County, New York, in January 1888 because of his interest in Claverack's military training program.

The Claverack experience was idyllic for Crane. He would later characterize it as the happiest period in his life. Although Crane never read deeply or widely, he had his most intense period of exposure to the classics and to nineteenth-century English and American literature at Claverack. He had youthful flirtations, and he contributed his first signed article, a two-column sketch on the exploits of Henry M. Stanley, to the school's magazine, *Vidette*. During summers he helped his brother Townley collect society gossip along the New Jersey shore for his Asbury Park news agency. Crane's studies were eclectic. Students of the three-year classical or academic programs at Claverack were prepared to enter the third year of college. Although Crane initially enrolled in the classical program, he later apparently switched to the academic curriculum; however, he did not follow the requirements for the program closely, for when he entered Lafayette College in fall 1890, having completed two and a half years at Claverack, he was still only a freshman.

While at Claverack, Crane seriously considered a military career. Preparing himself for West Point, he rose rapidly in the ranks of the student battalion; however, his brother William, who had often entertained him with knowledgeable accounts of the Battles of Chancellorsville and Gettysburg, was convinced that there would be no war in Stephen's lifetime and that consequently he would not prosper as an army officer. Searching for a more practical career, he transferred into Lafayette College's mining-engineering program. He left Claverack sadly but with fond memories. Shortly after arriving at Lafayette, he wrote to a Claverack classmate, "So you are not having a hell of a time at C. C., eh? Well, you had better have it now because, mark my words, you will always regret the day you leave old C. C. The fellows here raise more hell than any college in the country, yet I have still left a big slice of my heart up among the pumpkin seeds and farmers of Columbia Co" (*Correspondence* 35).

At Lafayette, Crane joined the Delta Upsilon fraternity, played intramural baseball, and roomed by himself in the rear of East Hall, where, according to Ernest G. Smith of the class of 1894, he terrified a group of hazing sophomores who broke down his door by confronting them with a revolver (*Log* 52–53). Crane received grades in four courses for the term ending in December: 60 in algebra, 88 in French, 92 in elocution, and 0 in theme writing. (The "themes" would have had to be on his technical area of specialization and not general subjects.) His excessive absences probably prevented his being graded in other courses. After the Christmas holidays he returned briefly to Lafayette, although the semester was over. Despite his academic deficiencies, he was not, as is often stated, asked to leave the college. He transferred at the insistence of his mother, who believed that as the grand nephew of Bishop Jesse Truesdell Peck, one of the founders of Syracuse University, Stephen was entitled to a scholarship at the Methodist institution.

Stephen stayed briefly with the Bishop's widow before moving into the Delta Upsilon house at Syracuse. He registered as a science major but by the end of the semester had earned only a single grade, an A in English literature. Rather than attending classes regularly, he spent much of the time playing baseball, socializing with friends, as well as interviewing criminals and prostitutes in the local police court and exploring the shabby entertainment district of the city as a correspondent for the *New York Tribune*. These experiences in the seedy life of Syracuse may have led in spring 1891 to a first draft of what would later become his first significant work, *Maggie: A Girl of the Streets*. His most memorable piece of journalism at the time was a literary hoax, "Great Bugs in Onondaga," which appeared in the *Tribune* on June 1, 1891. Crane reported with mock seriousness that a locomotive carrying limestone from nearby quarries was halted by a swarm of huge bugs that exploded with crackling sounds as their armorlike shells were crushed under the wheels. As at Lafayette, Crane's departure from Syracuse University seems to have been entirely voluntary rather than at the suggestion of the administration. By spring 1891, he had determined to forego any further schooling and, after having "recovered from college" (*Correspondence* 163, n. 4), he decided to pursue a career as a writer.

NEW YORK CITY

Crane spent summer 1891 working for his brother Townley's news agency in Asbury Park. In August he met Hamlin Garland, who was presenting a lecture series on American literature at nearby Avon-by-the-Sea, and reported on Garland's lecture on William Dean Howells for the *New York Tribune.* The time with Garland was a turning point in Crane's career, for it introduced him to Garland's and Howells's view of literary realism. By the fall he was living closer to New York City in Lake View, New Jersey, with his brother Edmund, which allowed him to explore the slums of lower Manhattan. That December his mother died, and Stephen made Edmund his guardian.

The following summer Crane was back in Asbury Park working for his brother. Any hope that he might continue this seasonal employment ended abruptly, however, when he was fired by the *Tribune* for writing an article satirizing a local parade. In fall 1892 Crane moved into a rooming house at 1064 Avenue A in Manhattan inhabited by a group of medical students; Crane named the house the Pendennis Club. Here he could be close to the center of the newspaper world of New York City and the Bowery, the rowdy, glittering Broadway of the lower East Side with its dime museums, brothels, flop houses, and dance halls. Immersing himself into the Bowery ambiance, he revised the manuscript of *Maggie,* which was printed in late February–early March 1893. Though the reading public barely noticed it, Howells and Garland recognized Crane's literary genius in it.

Nearly penniless, Crane lived in poverty with artist and illustrator friends in various New York City tenements. One of these was Corwin Knapp Linson, a painter and magazine illustrator who had studied in Paris, whom Crane had met shortly before the publication of *Maggie.* While staying in Linson's studio in spring 1893, he planned to write a potboiler to make quick money. He happened to leaf through old copies of the *Century Magazine* and noticed the series "Battles and Leaders of the Civil War," which included graphic accounts of the Battle of Chancellorsville, and another series, "Recollections of a Private." Recognizing that the articles focused on facts and military details, he said to Linson, "'I wonder that some of those fellows don't tell how they *felt* in those scraps. They spout enough of what they *did,* but they're as emotionless as rocks'" (Linson, "Little Stories," 19). Thus was planted the seed for *The Red Badge of Courage.* He spent most of the summer at his brother Edmund's home in Lake View, working on the war novel. When he returned to New York in October, he moved into one of the large studios of the old Needham Building on East 23rd Street with several young artists and illustrators who had remained there after the Art Students League moved to 57th Street. Crane described the building as "a place of slumberous corridors rambling in puzzling turns and curves" that "once contained about all that was real in the Bohemian quality of New York" (*Works* 8: 313). Here and in other studios and lofts where he lived temporarily, Crane completed *The Red Badge* and wrote much of the poetry for his first collection of verse, *The Black Riders and Other Lines.* He fictionalized his bohemian life among the "Indians," his epithet for his roommates, in *The Third Violet* and in two sketches, "Stories Told by an Artist" and "The Silver Pageant." It was a poverty-stricken, but essentially carefree, existence. Crane told Hamlin Garland that "they all slept on the floor, dined off buns and sardines, and painted on towels or wrapping paper for lack of canvas" (Garland, *Roadside Meetings* 192). Frequently, Crane's poverty made it necessary for him to retreat to Hartwood, a tiny village in Sullivan County where his brother Edmund had bought a house in spring 1894. It was the closest thing to a home Crane would have during his adult years in America.

In December, *The Red Badge of Courage* appeared in an abridged version in several newspapers. Between January and May 1895 Crane traveled through the West and Mexico to write feature articles for the Bacheller, Johnson, and Bacheller syndicate. In May, *The Black Riders and Other Lines* appeared; later in the fall, with the book publication of *The Red Badge* in America and England, he became an international celebrity.

For the next several months, Crane was lionized as an important new star in the American literary sky. The best known—and most controversial—incident honoring him occurred in December 1895. Elbert Hubbard, a self-aggrandizing entrepreneur who had helped to start *The Philistine: A Periodical of Protest,* quickly set up a paper organization called the Society of the Philistines to arrange a banquet in Buffalo, New York, honoring Crane. Hubbard invited writers and journalists from around the country, though a number of them sent regrets, in all likelihood suspecting that Hubbard was primarily attempting to publicize the event and his own publishing ventures. Unfortunately, the banquet degenerated into a fiasco as attendees treated it as a roast and heckled and ridiculed Crane and other speakers. Although Crane was disillusioned by the experience and felt he had been used, he tried to take the incident in stride. Hubbard, however, exploited the event to the utmost. He printed a commemorative pamphlet, *A Souvenir and a Medley,* that reprinted favorable newspaper accounts of the banquet; regrets from those who could not attend; a previously published, sentimentalized view of Crane by Hubbard; and several short pieces, also mostly previously published by Crane.

Besides the embarrassment caused by the Philistine banquet, Crane received additional attention when the publication of *The Black Riders and Other Lines* created a lively debate over his startling treatment of poetic form and theme. Though some critics compared Crane favorably to Whitman, Nietzsche, and Dickinson, others ridiculed his technique, occasionally writing parodies. By 1896, therefore, Crane had discovered that fame often comes with a cost. Interestingly, his correspondence at this time was the most revealing he would write as he tried to sort out the personal and professional consequences of what it means to be a celebrity. In a letter sent in January 1896 apparently responding to questions about his literary career, Crane told John Northern Hilliard, editor of the *Rochester Post Express,* that

> The one thing that deeply pleases me in my literary life—brief and inglorious as it is—is the fact that men of sense believe me to be sincere. "Maggie," published in paper covers, made me the friendship of Hamlin Garland and W. D. Howells, and the one thing that makes my life worth living in the midst of all this abuse and ridicule is the consciousness that never for an instant have those friendships at all diminished. Personally I am aware that my work does not amount to a string of dried beans— I always calmly admit it. But I also know that I do the best that is in me, without regard to cheers or damnation. When I was the mark for every humorist in the country I went ahead, and now, when I am the mark for only 50 per cent of the humorists of the country, I go ahead, for I understand that a man is born into the world with his own pair of eyes and he is not at all responsible for his quality of personal honesty.
>
> To keep close to my honesty is my supreme ambition. There is a sublime egotism in talking of honesty. I, however, do not say that I am honest. I merely say that I am as nearly honest as a weak mental machinery will allow. This aim in life struck me as being the only thing worth while. A man is sure to fail at it, but there is something in the failure. (*Correspondence* 195-96)

At the same time that he wrote similarly sounding letters to other journalists asking about his life and career, he began corresponding with Nellie Crouse, a proper young woman from Ohio whom he had met only once at a tea party in New York City in January 1895. Though her letters to Crane have not survived, his seven letters, written between December 1895 and March 1896, do. Unlike any other letters written by him, they raise intriguing questions about his personality. Although he was attracted to her, he waited almost a year after their only meeting to write, perhaps feeling insecure and waiting until he had become famous. The letters are filled with self-conscious posturing and awkward declarations of moral principles such as the following:

> So you think I am successful? Well I dont [*sic*] know. Most people consider me successful. At least, they seem to so think. But upon my soul I have lost all appetite for victory, as victory is defined by the mob. I will be glad if I can feel on my death-bed that my life has been just and kind according to my ability and that every particle of my little ridiculous stock of eloquence and wisdom has been applied for the benefit of my kind. From this moment to that deathbed may be a short time or a long one but at any rate it means a life of labor and sorrow. I do not confront it blithely. I confront it with desperate resolution. (*Correspondence* 186)

Although Nellie responded initially with long letters and a photograph, her interest in Crane waned, causing him to write one last time about his "flagons of despair" (208). Were Crane's statements about his feelings and career to a woman he barely knew totally honest, or was he simply trying to figure out what to say to impress her? When he described himself as "a wild shaggy barbarian" and she responded that she preferred a more conventional person, he immediately changed his position: "your recent confession that in your heart you like the man of fashion more than you do some other kinds of men came nearer to my own view than perhaps you expected" (198, 200). Or is it possible that there is truth on both sides: that the bohemian youth who had felt comfortable exploring the seedy life of the city was also seeking respectability in middle-class society?

Whatever the answer, Crane still saw the advantage of at least posing as a bohemian "barbarian" as he explored the city for literary and journalistic purposes. In spring 1896 he began to investigate the Tenderloin District of New York City, the area between Fifth and Ninth Avenues from Madison Square to 49th Street. Like the Bowery, the Tenderloin was cluttered with theaters, saloons, gambling dens, and bordellos. Because of an extensive system of bribery, illegal activities operated under police protection. The area was named *Tenderloin* by Police Inspector Alexander "Clubber" Williams, who, when transferred from a quiet precinct to this area of graft and vice, supposedly quipped, "I've been having chuck steak ever since I've been on the force, and now I'm going to have a bit of tenderloin" (Mencken 197, n. 57).

By the fall, Crane was writing a series of feature articles about the Tenderloin for William Randolph Hearst's *New York Journal*. On the evening of September 16, Crane interviewed two chorus girls and Dora

Clark, a known streetwalker, for the series. While Crane escorted one of the chorus girls to a cable car, the two other women were falsely arrested for soliciting. When Crane returned, the other chorus girl said that he was her husband. To protect her, he agreed with her statement. Although the arresting officer released her, he took Dora Clark to the police station and incarcerated her. When Crane accompanied them and tried to make a formal statement about her innocence, a sergeant advised him not to get involved because he might ruin his reputation. As Crane wrote in "Adventures of a Novelist," an autobiographical article about the incident, "Apparently the united wisdom of the world declared that no man should do anything but throw his sense of justice to the winds in an affair of this description. 'Let a man have a conscience for the daytime,' said wisdom. 'Let him have a conscience for the daytime, but it is idiocy for a man to have a conscience at 2:30 in the morning, in the case of an arrested prostitute'" (*Prose* 869-70).

Crane suffered dearly for following his conscience. Though newspapers initially praised his bravery, the police began a campaign of harassment against him. When they invaded his apartment and found supplies for smoking opium mounted on a wall plaque, they threatened to arrest him for running an opium den if he testified on behalf of Dora Clark. (The supplies were actually mementos of a detailed study of opium addiction that Crane had published in 1896.) Nonetheless, Crane did testify, and as a result his reputation was irreparably tarnished with false accusations of immorality and drug addiction. The incident also ended Crane's friendship with Theodore Roosevelt, then chairman of the Board of Police Commissioners. Realizing that his career in New York City as a writer and reporter was finished, he took an assignment offer from the Bacheller newspaper syndicate to travel to Cuba to cover the growing insurrection against Spanish rule.

FLORIDA AND THE *COMMODORE,* GREECE

In late November 1896, Crane arrived in Jacksonville, Florida, en route to Cuba to report on the growing rebellion against Spanish rule for the Bacheller newspaper syndicate. His plan was to arrange a secret voyage on one of the boats that were smuggling arms to the insurgents in Cuba and somehow send back news dispatches on whatever he discovered. To maintain his secrecy, a special concern given his fame and notoriety following the Dora Clark incident in New York City a month earlier, he registered at a local hotel as "Samuel Carleton." Soon, however, a local newspaper interviewed him and reported that "the representative of a syndicate of Northern newspapers" (*Log* 232) was headed for Cuba.

Crane soon began an affair with Cora Howorth Murphy Stewart, who operated a house of pleasure, the Hotel de Dream, under the cognomen of Taylor. At the time, Cora was unhappily married to her second husband, an aristocratic British soldier named Captain Donald William Stewart, who was on colonial service in Africa and who refused to divorce her. For the next few weeks, Stephen and Cora stayed together. Thirty-one years old to Crane's 25, she was a cultured woman with literary interests. Despite the intensity of their relationship, Crane spent much of his time in Jacksonville playing poker at a local hotel and frequenting taverns with other journalists hoping to sail to Cuba.

Crane would certainly have been aware of how dangerous an attempt to sneak into Cuba would be. Spanish gunboats had orders to capture or destroy filibusters attempting to reach there. If an American journalist made it to shore but got captured, he would have been imprisoned, for the Spanish considered American journalists to be spies. Though there had been stories of journalists who had been incarcerated and tortured, Crane seemed unconcerned about possible danger. Before he left Jacksonville, he wrote that "we are troubled occasionally by Spanish spies ... [though] they seem very harmless" (*Correspondence* 271).

On New Year's Eve Crane sailed on the filibustering steamship *Commodore,* which was carrying guns and ammunition, a crew, and Cuban guerrillas. Because journalists were officially barred from entering Cuba, he signed on as a crew member. Although the ship was violating U.S. neutrality laws by being a filibuster, the secretary of the treasury had cleared it and its contents in all likelihood because of growing American sentiment for the rebellion against Spanish occupation of Cuba. Two miles down the St. John's River and in heavy fog, the boat ran aground and had to wait until daylight to be pulled from the mud. On its second trip out, the boat was beached again but eventually freed itself. On the evening of January 1, however, a leak was discovered, and the boat came to a standstill about 18 miles off the coast. By early next morning, the captain gave the order to abandon ship. Three lifeboats left the vessel. Two reached the shore, but when the third one foundered, the seven men on it returned to the *Commodore* and built makeshift rafts. One of the men died while leaping toward a raft and plunging into the sea; three men were still on board when the ship sank; and the other three lost their lives on the rafts. The captain, a cook, an oiler, and Crane were the last to leave the ship in a ten-foot dinghy. They drifted alongside the *Commodore* until it went down and attempted to save the men on the rafts. For almost the next 30 hours, they battled heavy seas until the dinghy capsized in the surf near Daytona Beach. The oiler drowned before reaching the shore, and an onlooker dragged the other three exhausted men from the breakers. Crane's harrowing experience of near death was literally front-page news with such headlines as "Filibuster Sunk—Crane Missing" (*New York Press,* January 3, 1897, pp. 1, 2) and "Young New York Writer Astonishes the Sea Dogs by His Courage in the Face of Death" (*New York Press,* January 4, 1897, pp. 1, 2).

By January 4, Crane was back in Jacksonville writing a newspaper report of the sinking, "Stephen Crane's Own Story," which appeared in the *New York Press* on January 7. He also began working on what would become his most famous short story, "The Open Boat," a fictional account of the experience from his point of view. Later, he wrote a related piece, "Flanagan and His Short Filibustering Adventure," told from the point of view of a captain.

After unsuccessfully attempting to find another ship to take him to Cuba in February, Crane signed with the *New York Journal* as a correspondent to report on the impending Greek-Turkish War and persuaded the newspaper to send Cora with him as one of the first female war correspondents. Though Crane had effectively depicted combat in *The Red Badge of Courage* without ever having firsthand knowledge of it, the experience of war in Greece, as he later told Joseph Conrad, proved to him that his war novel was "all right" (Conrad 11). The brief, month-long struggle evolved into a series of retreats and rearguard actions on the part of the Greeks and ended in their complete humiliation. Although he found combat curiously exhilarating, he also reported its tragic consequences. In "Stephen Crane Tells of War's Horrors," he reported the terrible plight of 800 wounded troops crammed on board a hospital ship: "There is more of this sort of thing in war than glory and heroic death, flags, banners, shouting and victory" (*Prose* 942). In addition to his war dispatches, he captured the vagaries of war in "Death and the Child," one of his finest war stories. Following the end of the war, Stephen and Cora visited France for almost two weeks, then left for England, which would become their home until Crane's death in 1900.

RAVENSBROOK, ENGLAND

Crane's decision to move to England in June 1897 was prompted at least partly by his recognition that he could not easily return to

New York City, nor could he bring home to Hartwood or Port Jervis, New York—where his traditional, middle-class relatives lived—the "hostess" of a Jacksonville pleasure resort. Living at Ravensbrook, Oxted, Surrey, "Mr. and Mrs. Crane" were near Harold Frederic, Ford Madox Ford, and H. G. Wells, who were also living with women not their wives. To conceal his location and affair with Cora from his family, Crane listed his English publisher rather than Ravensbrook as his return address in letters to his brothers. The Cranes opened their doors to many visitors, and Stephen wrote some of his finest stories, including "The Bride Comes to Yellow Sky," "The Blue Hotel," and "The Monster." Despite literary friendships, public adulation, and artistic success, however, Crane gradually became restless and found himself increasingly in debt brought on by his and Cora's extravagance. During the summer and fall, he considered traveling as a correspondent, perhaps to the Sudan or the Klondike. He got his opportunity when the United States officially recognized Cuba's independence from Spain in April 1898. Quickly sailing from England to New York City, he signed a contract with Joseph Pulitzer's *New York World* and headed for Florida to join other correspondents in Key West and Tampa awaiting the impending invasion of Cuba.

CUBA

Although Crane and many other correspondents spent much of May 1898 in dispatch boats off the coast of Cuba looking for news of the American navy's intentions, he soon was directly involved in combat and covered the landings at Guantánamo, the advance on Las Guásimas, and the Battle of San Juan Hill. Two controversial incidents, however, got him in trouble with Pulitzer. When Crane learned that Edward Marshall, his friend and rival correspondent, had been wounded, he supervised his removal to a field hospital and then walked several miles through arduous terrain to cable Marshall's dispatch to his newspaper, William Randolph Hearst's *New York Journal*, the *World's* main competitor. The second incident involved the behavior of the 71st New York Regiment at the Battle of San Juan Hill. On July 16, the *World* published an unsigned front-page article criticizing the regiment's disorganized and confused performance during the battle. The next day, when the rival *Journal* reprinted the *World* article under the headline "Slurs on the Bravery of the Boys of the 71st.," the *World* immediately responded with stories and editorials praising the regiment and started an unsuccessful campaign to raise money to erect a monument to its fallen men. When Crane returned to the United States in July because of malaria, the business manager of the *World* accused him of writing the article and of not reporting the war; however, the charges were false, prompted most likely by the manager's dislike of Crane and Crane's filing Marshall's dispatch to a rival newspaper. Rather than shirking his duty, Crane had published about two dozen war dispatches, and all the evidence suggests that another correspondent wrote the article criticizing the regiment. When Crane visited the editorial office of the *World,* he argued with the manager about the accusations against him and was quickly fired, whereupon he accepted an offer from the *New York Journal* to cover the Puerto Rican campaign of the Spanish-American War.

After the war ended in August, Crane disappeared into Havana for the next several months, during which he filed dispatches to the *Journal,* wrote poetry, and completed most of the Cuban War stories that were to compose *Wounds in the Rain* (1900); however, he corresponded with practically no one and did not tell his family and friends—especially an increasingly frantic Cora—where he was. Finally succumbing to growing debts and family pressure, Crane sailed for New York in late December and by January was in England.

BREDE PLACE, ENGLAND

Reunited with Cora, they faced more than a year's worth of unpaid bills that almost left them bankrupt. With the help of legal advice and loans from friends and family, they tried to start life anew at Brede Place, a medieval manor house in Brede, Sussex, where Crane wrote incessantly to try to remain solvent. In 1899 he published three volumes: *War Is Kind,* his second collection of poems; *Active Service,* a novel about the Greek-Turkish War; and *The Monster and Other Stories,* which contains a largely unknown masterpiece, "The Monster," about middle-class hypocrisy. He also worked on a number of other projects including *Whilomville Stories* (1900), stories about children; *Wounds in the Rain* (1900), stories about the Cuban War; *Great Battles of the World* (1901), a series of articles about major battles; and an adventurous romance titled *The O'Ruddy* (1903), which was completed by his friend Robert Barr after Crane's death.

Crane's correspondence during his time at Brede Place makes clear that he was writing as rapidly as he could to pay bills, though "his great difficulty," Cora wrote to a friend, "is the lack of that machine-like application which makes a man work steadily" (*Correspondence* 413). With bills coming in almost daily, he continually asked his literary agent for advances, on one occasion dealt with one agent behind the back of another, promised them a steady stream of stories, and routinely reduced his writing to word counts that allowed him to compute how much a publisher would owe him. To one agent, he desperately wrote in August 1899, "I must have altogether within the next ten days £150—no less, as the Irish say. But, by the same token, I am going to earn it—mainly, in Whilomville Stories for they are sure and quick money. £40 of my £150 have I done yesterday and today but for all your gods, help me or I perish" (494). Days later, he wrote again, "I am sending you another of the Whilomville stories for Harper and Bros. It is 4095 words and for it they will pay you (at $50 per thousand) something over forty pounds. Please send me £30 by next post. I need it badly" (494). In an article aptly titled "The Dollars Damned Him," A.J. Liebling concluded that Crane "died ... of the cause most common among American middle-class males—anxiety about money" (18).

In one sense, Brede Place, with its damp air and its lack of electricity and modern plumbing, was an awful location for Crane, who had not completely recovered from malaria contracted in Cuba. Nonetheless, he enjoyed living like an English squire with his dogs at his side and a house staff to serve him. Although the Cranes welcomed visits from nearby literary friends—for example, Henry James, Joseph Conrad, Ford Madox Ford, and Edward Garnett—they often found their home, as was the case at Ravensbrook, filled with unwanted guests taking advantage of their friendliness. Their lavish lifestyle and inability to manage funds also caused problems daily.

Despite their money problems, the Cranes hosted an elaborate four-day Christmas party for 50–60 guests at Brede Place in 1899 that featured the production of a dramatic farce, *The Ghost*, based upon the legend of the Brede ghost, Sir Goddard Oxenbridge. Crane solicited snippets of dialogue from his literary friends and incorporated them into the farce, which was produced for the only time on December 28. After the ball the following evening, Crane collapsed with a lung hemorrhage. Although the doctor offered hope for recovery, Crane's health declined rapidly. In April 1900 he suffered another massive hemorrhage that incapacitated him entirely. As a final effort, plans were made to get Crane to Badenweiler, Germany, for the Nordrach cure, a treatment for consumption based on sanatorium rest coordinated with mild exercise, overfeeding, and pure air.

A few days after arriving in Badenweiler at the end of May, Crane experienced severe hemorrhaging again and was given an injection of morphine. He sank into a coma and died on June 5. Distraught and exhausted, Cora jotted down disjointed notes that suggest she feared that the injection was a mistake:

> Write to Dr Skinner about Morphine—
> —"Thats [sic] what strayed him"—
> "You can cut them she cant [sic]."
> "Little Butcher, I will tell Skinner how he came to Bali & stole me"—
> To nurse: "Did you know Dr Bruce never heard of him?" Dr called June 4th 8 P.M—Gave morphine injection—went at once to heart, I could see by muscular contraction Dr. saw too, tried to give champhor injection to revive action of heart. Dr said next day: "Can you forgive me?" What did he mean? don't dare to think.
>
> (*Log* 443-44)

Upon hearing of Crane's untimely death, friends, reporters, and journalists throughout Europe and America mourned the loss of such a great writer. Fellow journalists who had reported on the Spanish-American War with him adopted a resolution recognizing Crane as a "brilliant journalist and gifted author.... We admired his genius and loved him as a man. We shall cherish his memory always" (*Log* 445). Edward Marshall, who had originally hired Crane to write for the *New York Press* in 1894, wrote that "in losing Crane America lost one of her most promising young writers. But his friends lost more. They lost a chap whom they all knew to be a real man as well as a talented acquaintance" (8). To the *London Spectator,* Crane was "a writer of singular force and originality, whose studies in the psychology of peril had the clairvoyance nothing short of magical" (Stallman, *Biography* 561). Of all the tributes, eulogies, and regrets recorded, none captures the sadness of Crane's death more poignantly than Henry James's words to Cora: "What a brutal, needless extinction—what an unmitigated unredeemed catastrophe! I think of him with such a sense of possibilities and powers!" (*Log* 446)

Literary Heritage

Stephen Crane was born into one of the most dramatic periods in American history. Following the Civil War, the country changed dramatically in terms of size, population, and economy. In addition to these changes, two new literary movements, Realism and later Naturalism, were replacing Romanticism. By the time that Crane was pursuing a writing career in the 1890s, the literary world was in the midst of what became known as the Realism War, as writers debated how best to write fiction. Crane would be strongly influenced by two writers central to the debate, Hamlin Garland and William Dean Howells.

AMERICA BEFORE THE CIVIL WAR

During the nineteenth century, America continued to expand westward so that by the 1850s it stretched from the Atlantic to the Pacific Ocean. Because of the wealth of natural resources and a firm belief in self-reliance, Americans thought optimistically about themselves and the future of their country. It was a place of rebirth in the development of civilization, a new Eden whose inhabitants had a manifest destiny to lead the world politically, militarily, and economically. To be sure, a Puritan heritage reminded many Americans of their own sinfulness, as seen in the dark vision of the soul in the fiction of Edgar Allan Poe, Nathaniel Hawthorne, and Herman Melville, but for others such as

Ralph Waldo Emerson, "the theological problems of original sin, origin of evil, predestination, and the like ... are the soul's mumps, and measles, and whooping-coughs" (Emerson 150); they are the illnesses that civilization will overcome as it matures with the guidance of American democracy. As George Bancroft wrote in his *History of the United States* (1834–76), "Every thing is in motion, and for the better" (Brooks, Lewis, and Warren 1202). From the point of view of Americans, as the country progressed, so too did civilization.

An important kind of fiction written at the time was the romance, which differed from the novel. As Hawthorne wrote in his preface to *The House of the Seven Gables* (1851), a novel "is presumed to aim at a very minute fidelity, not merely to the possible, but to the probable and ordinary course of man's experience," whereas a romance, while it must follow "the truth of the human heart—has fairly a right to present that truth under circumstances, to a great extent, of the writer's own choosing or creation. If he think fit, he may so manage his atmospherical medium as to bring out or mellow the lights and deepen and enrich the shadows of the picture" (Hawthorne 243). Hawthorne's *The Scarlet Letter* (1850), one of the best examples of a romance, dramatizes the psychological impact caused by the concealment of sin. Although the story is set in Puritan Boston in the mid-seventeenth century, its symbolic treatment of pride, hidden guilt, and conscience transcends time and place as forces of good and evil confront each other. Because Hawthorne was writing a romance, he captured "the truth of the human heart" but felt no need to limit the plot to "probable and ordinary" events. For example, when a meteor illuminates the cloudy sky, people see a "great red letter ... the letter A" (176). For the sexton, the A means *Angel* to commemorate the death of Governor Winthrop, but for Reverend Dimmesdale, "another's guilt might have seen another symbol in it" (178, 176). Although a meteor is a natural occurrence, it is highly unlikely that it would form a recognizable letter in the sky. A writer of romance, however, does not feel bound by how nature typically works. In the romance world of *The Scarlet Letter,* nature is part of an ethical universe in which all events have a significance for humanity. Thus, the A in the sky is nature's symbolic way of simultaneously acknowledging the death of a leader and reminding Dimmesdale of his moral transgression. Similarly, Herman Melville's *Moby-Dick* (1851) is ostensibly a story about American seamen searching for a whale in the Atlantic Ocean, but on a deeper level it is, like *The Scarlet Letter,* a romance about the problem of evil in the universe.

AMERICA AFTER THE CIVIL WAR

Before the Civil War, America was largely a land of farms and villages with few cities. This soon changed, however, with the sudden growth of cities. Whereas in 1860 600,000 people lived in New York City, by 1900 the number had increased to more than 3,000,000. The change in Chicago was even more dramatic: a population of 30,000 in 1861 had grown to over 1,000,000 by the end of the century. Many of the new inhabitants—the "huddled masses" welcomed in Emma Lazarus's poetic tribute to the Statue of Liberty, "The New Colossus" (1883)— were immigrants who came to America as the land of opportunity. By 1890 New York had twice as many Jews as Warsaw, Poland; twice as many Irish as Dublin, Ireland; and the same number of Germans as Hamburg, Germany (Lee 4). Overall, during the second half of the nineteenth century, urban populations quadrupled.

The dramatic growth in population mirrored the expansion of the country itself. During the Civil War, Kansas, Nevada, and West Virginia became states, and in 1867 Alaska was purchased from Russia for 2¢ an acre. In 1889 Montana, South Dakota, North Dakota, and Washington were admitted as states, followed by Idaho and Wyoming in 1890 and Utah in 1896. In the treaty ending the Spanish-American War in 1898, America took control of the Philippines, Guam, and Puerto Rico and annexed Hawaii. Other changes reflected the way people traveled. In New York City the completion of an elevated railroad system in 1881 and the Brooklyn Bridge, the largest suspension bridge in the world when it was completed in 1883, linked residents more efficiently. More dramatic were changes in transportation from coast to coast. With the completion of the Central Pacific and Union Pacific transcontinental railroads in 1869; the Northern Pacific and the Atchison, Topeka, and Santa Fe railroads in 1883; and the adoption of a standard time by all railroads in the same year, Americans could travel across the continent in days rather than weeks.[1]

Just as dramatic was the realization of the American success story of self-made millionaires. In 1861 there were fewer than 100 millionaires in the country, but by 1876 there were more than 1,000. Seven years later the number had increased to about 4,000. The American dream of personal success was being played out by such men as John Jacob Astor, Andrew Carnegie, Henry Frick, Jay Gould, J. P. Morgan, John D. Rockefeller, and Cornelius Vanderbilt and was portrayed as being divinely sanctioned. As Bishop Lawrence of Massachusetts proclaimed, "Godliness is in league with riches. . . . Material prosperity is helping to make the national character sweeter, more joyous, more unselfish, more Christlike" (Brooks, Lewis, and Warren 1202). Such statements reflected the kind of thinking made famous by Carnegie in his essay "The Gospel of Wealth," setting forth the idea that the wealthy should live unpretentiously and help the less fortunate; thus, Carnegie gave large amounts of money to libraries and educational institutions throughout the United States.

Although the period following the Civil War was marked by optimism about the future of America, there was a dark side to paradise. The war may have ended slavery, but racism was pervasive. The end of Reconstruction in 1877 and the Supreme Court decision of *Plessy v. Ferguson* in 1896 kept African Americans as second-class citizens. Native Americans met their final defeat in the Massacre at Wounded Knee in 1890, following decades of mistreatment, broken promises by dishonest white agents, and the loss of homeland. Though Chinese workers were initially welcomed in America, white laborers fearing loss of jobs attacked them, and in 1883 the Chinese Exclusion Act prohibited Chinese from immigrating here. Labor disputes led to violent conflict in the Chicago Haymarket Square Riot in 1886 and the Homestead, Pennsylvania, steel strike in 1892. A volatile economy led to financial panic, a stock market crash, and a financial depression that left many impoverished. Because the government maintained a laissez-faire attitude toward big business, the temptation of corruption was widespread. Robber Barons, as ruthless businessmen came to be called, bribed public officials, swindled people, and crushed labor disputes with violent force. Appalled by the greed and hypocrisy, Edward Bellamy, in his utopian novel *Looking Backward: 2000–1887* (1888), contrasted the moral decline of the country with an idealized version of America where everyone is treated fairly and equally. The most influential utopian novel in America, it spawned clubs to discuss ways to implement its ideas to improve society. The novel best remembered for its depiction of post–Civil War America also gave the period its best-known title: *The Gilded Age* (1873) by Mark Twain and Charles Dudley Warner. Like a gilded object, America was, for Twain and Warner, cheap and tawdry beneath its exterior of gold and glitter. In the story, a newspaper editor comments, "We are reminded of a note which we received from the notorious burglar Murphy, in which he finds fault with a statement of ours to the effect that he has served one term in the penitentiary and also one in the U.S. Senate. He says, 'The latter statement is untrue and does me great injustice'" (Twain 422).

REALISM

During this time American literature saw the rise of two new literary movements, Realism and Naturalism, which were partly a reaction against Romanticism. Broadly defined, Realism is a literary technique that aims for verisimilitude, in other words, a reliable representation of reality. In Hawthorne's terms, as he described in his preface to *The House of the Seven Gables,* it was the kind of writing that aimed "at a very minute fidelity, not merely to the possible, but to the probable and ordinary course of man's experience." Among its major practitioners were William Dean Howells, Hamlin Garland, and Mark Twain.

Its popularity reflected a renewed interest in science and technology. Scientists were the new American heroes. In *Famous Americans of Recent Times* (1868), James Parton devoted a third of his book to them (Carter 91). By observing nature closely and accurately and by applying science to the solving of everyday problems in society, they invented ways to improve life—such as the Bessemer process to convert iron to steel commercially in 1864, the patenting of the telephone in 1876, or the first skeleton-frame skyscraper in Chicago in 1885. Like scientists, realists observed society closely and treated fiction as a laboratory in which to examine it. In Mark Twain's *A Connecticut Yankee in King Arthur's Court,* for example, Hank Morgan is the pragmatic observer who uses nineteenth-century science and technology to confront superstition and falsehood in sixth-century England. Just as scientists wanted to improve the physical well-being of society, realists wanted to improve its moral well-being.

Though not all realists professed the same set of beliefs, most adhered to the following characteristics:

1. The novelist recreates the external world as accurately as possible, with special attention to the physical details of clothing, landscape, architecture, and a person's face.
2. The characters are common people in the present day rather than from long ago and far away and deal with everyday problems.
3. Character development is emphasized rather than plot.
4. The action does not rely on sentimentality and melodrama and is often the result of complex ethical choices. As Howells said, "Morality penetrates all things, it is the soul of all things" (Carter 390).
5. Dialect reflects a character's cultural and geographical roots.
6. In trying to be objective, narrators avoid moralizing about characters.

THE RISE OF SILAS LAPHAM (1885)

A classic example of a realistic novel is William Dean Howells's *The Rise of Silas Lapham* (1885). Silas Lapham, a rural farmer from Vermont, has risen in prominence and moved to Boston after making a fortune as a paint manufacturer. He begins to build a mansion and starts to establish his family in high society. When he makes risky financial decisions, however, he is faced with bankruptcy. His only hope is to sell a milling property to an English syndicate, even though he knows that the sale will irreparably damage the syndicate. Faced with a moral dilemma—should he deceive the syndicate so that he can keep his wealth?—he maintains his sense of integrity, though it ruins him financially and forces him to move his family back to Vermont.

As is typical in a realistic novel, details about appearance and speech pattern help to bring a character alive. Silas

> is a fine type of the successful American. He has a square, bold chin, only partially concealed by the short reddish-grey beard, growing to the edges of his firmly closing lips. His nose is short and straight; his forehead good, but broad rather than high; his eyes blue, and with a light in them that is kindly or sharp according to his mood. He is of medium height, and fills an average arm-chair with a solid bulk, which on the day of our interview was unpretentiously clad in a business suit of blue serge. His head droops somewhat from a short neck, which does not trouble itself to rise far from a pair of massive shoulders. (Howells, *Rise* 6)

Despite his success as a businessman, his formal education has been limited. Silas's speech, for example, reveals his ignorance about grammar and pronunciation. When discussing a popular French style of decorative arts in the early nineteenth century, he mispronounces *Empire* ['äm-"pir] as "Ongpeer," and when he decides to build his mansion despite his wife's objections, he declares, "I guess the ayes has it, Pen," said her father. "How would it do to let Irene and your mother stick in the old place here, and us go into the new house?" To which the narrator tells the reader, "At times the Colonel's grammar failed him" (41, 37).

Though there is a clear plot and subplot, the focus is on character development. When the story begins, Silas has already made his fortune and has thus already risen materially. Like Carnegie, Rockefeller, or Vanderbilt, he is a self-made man. Had Howells been more interested in action, he could have shown how Silas went from rags to riches with adventures along the way. This would have been the method of a novelist interested only in melodrama, sentimentality, and pure adventure. Realists, however, were less concerned with what happens to people and more interested in how their choices affect their lives, especially in terms of ethical behavior. Rich and famous, Silas decides that his worth can be measured by two things: acceptance of his family into upper-class society and the construction of a huge mansion in a posh section of Boston. Howells would have certainly been aware of how his story reflected real life. This was the time of "conspicuous consumption" and the construction of castlelike homes in America as ways of flaunting one's wealth. For example, in 1883, two years before the publication of Howells's novel, William H. Vanderbilt constructed a block-long, Italian Renaissance mansion at 52nd Street and Fifth Avenue for $3 million. Mrs. Alva Vanderbilt spent $250,000 on costumes, food, and decoration to host the most famous social event in New York history at which Mrs. Cornelius Vanderbilt, dressed as "The Electric Light," appeared in a white satin gown studded with diamonds. As with the Vanderbilts, Silas's identity and self-worth were defined by appearances. Faced with bankruptcy, he makes the right decision ethically not to cheat others and eventually realizes that though he has fallen financially, he has risen morally.

As a realistic writer, Howells treated fiction as a place to examine daily problems in his own society and to offer solutions. The specifics surrounding Silas—for example, that he made his fortune in paint or that he was building a mansion—are not so important as the fact that he was facing issues dealing with proper behavior and personal values in a burgeoning democracy. Though never losing sight that people can be mean and corrupt, realists generally believed in the essential goodness of humanity. Sin and corruption do exist, but with education and the inculcation of moral values society can continue to progress.

NATURALISM

Toward the end of the nineteenth century, a new school of writers, the naturalists, began to question the philosophical assumptions on which Realism was built. Central to Realism was a belief in a well-ordered universe in which humans have a free will that allows them to make right or wrong decisions. The biological determinism of Charles Darwin and the economic determinism of Karl Marx suggested, however, that the universe was controlled by forces greater than individuals: namely, heredity, environment, and chance. Because individuals have little, if any, free will, ethical questions about right or wrong are irrelevant. The universe is simply amoral. Among the writers drawn to Naturalism were Frank Norris, Theodore Dreiser, and Jack London.

As with Realism, there has been considerable debate about a precise definition of Naturalism because writers varied in their attitudes toward it; nevertheless, they believed in the following:

1. Characters seem to have little, if any, free will and are controlled by their heredity, instinct, and raw emotions or by social and economic forces beyond their control.
2. Under pressure, they act more like animals than intelligent human beings.
3. The strong survive; the weak do not.
4. Chance and fate control human events.
5. Nature is indifferent toward human actions.
6. Questions of morality are immaterial in an amoral universe.
7. Narrators treat their subject with candor and an almost scientific detachment.

MCTEAGUE (1899)

Frank Norris's *McTeague* (1899) is a classic example of Naturalism. McTeague is a physically strong but mentally weak dentist in San Francisco who marries Trina Sieppe. By chance, she wins $5,000 in a lottery. Rather than using the money to improve her and her husband's life, she becomes greedy and hoards it. Because their friend Schouler had hoped to marry Trina, he feels cheated out of the money. Out of revenge, he reveals to an authority that McTeague is practicing dentistry without a license or degree. The exposure forces McTeague to give up his business. When he and Trina become increasingly despondent, she continues to refuse to spend her money. He leaves her, steals some of the money, and in an attempt to get more kills her. He runs from the law and eventually ends up in Death Valley unexpectedly pursued by Schouler. McTeague kills him, but not before Schouler handcuffs their wrists together. The story ends with McTeague's dying of thirst, locked to the corpse of his nemesis.

Physical details are just as important to naturalists as they are to realists, but they depict humanity as primitive. McTeague, for example,

> was a young giant, carrying his huge shock of blond hair six feet three inches from the ground; moving his immense limbs, heavy with ropes of muscle, slowly, ponderously. His hands were enormous, red, and covered with a fell of stiff yellow hair; they were hard as wooden mallets, strong

as vises, the hands of the old-time car-boy. Often he dispensed with forceps and extracted a refractory tooth with his thumb and finger. His head was square-cut, angular; the jaw salient, like that of the carnivora.

McTeague's mind was as his body, heavy, slow to act, sluggish. Yet there was nothing vicious about the man. Altogether he suggested the draught horse, immensely strong, stupid, docile, obedient. (Norris 3-4)

Unlike characters in *The Rise of Silas Lapham,* McTeague, Trina, and Schouler do not act civilly under pressure, struggle with moral issues, and learn from their mistakes. Controlled by base passion, they act instinctively like violent animals. During a brutal fight, Schouler is "a snake spit[ting] its venom" (185) and bites through McTeague's ear, causing it to bleed.

Then followed a terrible scene. The brute that in McTeague lay so close to the surface leaped instantly to life, monstrous, not to be resisted. He sprang to his feet with a shrill and meaningless clamor, totally unlike the ordinary bass of his speaking tones. It was the hideous yelling of a hurt beast, the squealing of a wounded elephant. He framed no words; in the rush of high-pitched sound that issued from his wide-open mouth there was nothing articulate. It was something no longer human; it was rather an echo from the jungle. (185)

Had a realist written *McTeague,* he or she would not have overlooked the greed and jealousy that permeates it; however, there might have been moral growth. McTeague might have managed with another career, Schouler might have dealt with his anger, and Trina might have confronted her involvement in a dysfunctional marriage. Even if these three characters remained unchanged, there would have been a sense that not all people were like them. Norris makes clear, however, that they are not anomalies in society. Trina's incessant need to save money, for example, is the result of a "good deal of peasant blood [that] still ran undiluted in her veins, and she had all the instinct of a hardy and penurious mountain race—the instinct which saves without any thought, without idea of consequence—saving for the sake of saving, hoarding without knowing why" (106).

Whereas *The Rise of Silas Lapham* charts the efficacy of moral evolution in society, *McTeague* captures the amoral devolution of nature itself—"a vast, unconquered brute of the Pliocene epoch, savage, sullen, and magnificently indifferent to man" (298-99). Naturalism is a product of pessimism and cynicism—even at times of despair; it is Realism gone sour. Totally missing is any sense of a rational enlightenment, of a belief in the dignity and perfectibility of humanity, and of a general faith in democracy and the future of America. These are now empty dreams. Ironically, Naturalism in various forms would become the dominant literary movement in American literature in the twentieth century.

INFLUENCE OF HAMLIN GARLAND ON STEPHEN CRANE

Stephen Crane was attuned to the literary currents that flowed through America in the late nineteenth century. More than any of his contemporaries, he experimented with different literary techniques. At various times he was a realist, a naturalist, and an impressionist who blended humor, local color, and psychological portrayal that made him, as described by Daniel G. Hoffman, a "literary chameleon" (Hoffman, "First Story" 273). However, it is unclear what authors he read, though he was certainly well versed in the Bible and was at least familiar with major writers of classical, English, and American literature—for example, Homer, Shakespeare, and James Fenimore Cooper. Clearly, though, the two most influential writers on him as he learned his craft were Hamlin Garland and William Dean Howells. Both were important American authors who influenced the development of Realism.

Before meeting Garland, Crane was, like many an aspiring writer, struggling to find his own voice. As he later told his friend Corwin Knapp Linson, "when [I] first began to write [I] could hardly think of what to write about." In search of a social and literary identity, he experimented with different themes and literary forms in much of his early work. Whereas in one of his classroom exercises he romanticized about the heroic exploits of the British-American journalist Henry Stanley, in another exercise he ridiculed British imperialism. In terms of form, much of his early work was imitative as he experimented with the dramatic essay, the literary sketch, and the tall tale. The disciplined rigor of a traditional education, however, did not appeal to him, and after suffering through one year of what he called "the cut-and-dried curriculum of . . . college" (*Correspondence* 99), he left school for good in spring 1891. Though desirous of becoming a professional writer, he had no definite plan, no vision, no focus.

In summer 1891 Garland came to Avon-by-the-Sea, New Jersey, to give a series of lectures on American literature. Crane reported on the lecture on William Dean Howells for the *New York Tribune* and probably attended lectures on such other topics as local color, social contrasts, and the city in fiction. The following summer they renewed their acquaintance when Garland returned to Avon-by-the-Sea. Though he was amused by Crane's naïveté, he was impressed with his intellectual honesty and his zeal to be a writer.

Crane would have been especially attracted to Garland's publications around the time that they first met. Garland's 1891 collection of short stories, *Main-Travelled Roads,* was widely being praised for its honest portrayal of character, dialect, and setting, and his seaside lectures in 1891 and 1892 espoused a new theory of fiction that Garland then published as essays in two magazines, the *Arena* and *Forum,* and that were collected in *Crumbling Idols* in 1894. Though the actual texts of the lectures that Crane heard Garland deliver do not survive, in all likelihood they contained the spirit—if not the wording—of the published essays. Like Emerson's "The American Scholar" and Whitman's first preface to *Leaves of Grass, Crumbling Idols* was a literary manifesto that championed individual experience as a source of knowledge and guide to action; that called passionately for a new literature that would shed the chains imposed by literary tradition; and that would embrace the West, Garland's all-inclusive term for the rest of America, rather than the smug, conventional, Eastern literary establishment. Dedicating his book "to the men and women of America who have the courage to be artists," Garland articulated the classic tension between rebellious youth and conservative elders: "There come times in the development of every art when the creative mind re-asserts itself, and shakes itself loose from the terrible power of the past. This dissent, this demand for artistic freedom, is always made by youth, and always meets with the bitter and scornful opposition of the old. To conform is easy,—it is like sleep. To dissent is action in the interests of the minority" (Garland, *Crumbling Idols* 183). Garland encouraged his readers not to rely solely on schools for one's education, for they are

> conservative forces. They are nearly always linked with the aristocratic and the old, especially in their art instructions. Universities are bulwarks of tradition. They are pools left on the beach of an ebbing tide. They conserve the past. They study the living present but little. They are founded upon books. They teach conformity, they do not develop personality. (185)

For too long, schools have forced an aspiring essayist to imitate Addison; an aspiring novelist, Scott or Dickens; an aspiring dramatist, Shakespeare (11). These long-revered literary masters, these idols, were now crumbling, as do all idols. It was now time, Garland exhorted his readers, to "[a]ccept the battle challenge cheerfully, as those before you have done. What you win, you must fight for as of old. And remember, life and death both fight with you. Idols crumble and fall, but the skies lift their unmoved arch of blue, and the earth sends forth its rhythmic pulse of green, and in the blood of youth there comes the fever of rebellious art" (191–92). As Garland wrote in an 1892 essay, "The West in Literature," "Art, after all, is an individual thing. The advice I give to my pupils who are anxious to write is the essence of veritism: 'Write of those things of which you know most, and for which you care most. By so doing you will be true to yourself, true to your locality, and true to your time'" (676).

Garland's ideas in his lectures and essays resonated in Crane. During the next several years, Crane would echo Garland's thoughts—indeed, at times even Garland's words—in his private and public pronouncements. Just as Garland exhorted aspiring artists to "write of those things of which [they] know most," Crane "tried to observe closely, and to set down what I have seen in the simplest and most concise way" (*Correspondence* 230). And just as Garland rallied his followers in their battle against the "long-revered literary masters"—the "idols" as he called them—Crane declared in an 1894 letter to Lily Brandon Munroe that his early career was "more of a battle than a journey" as he fought against the literary forces that kept "Garland and I out of the big magazines" (63). As he told Lily, he had "developed all alone a little creed of art which I thought was a good one. Later I discovered that my creed was identical with the one of Howells and Garland" (63). It is more likely, however, that the pronouncement about his total originality as a writer was an attempt to impress her. Until Crane met Garland in 1891, he was an aspiring writer in search of his own distinctive literary voice whose literary production had mainly consisted of frivolous news items and imitative tales and sketches. For a struggling writer who had turned his back on college, who had been challenging established beliefs and institutions, and who would later describe his pursuit of a literary career as "a sincere, desperate, lonely battle to remain true to my conception of my life and the way it should be lived" (187), Garland's book and lectures were inspiring. In short, Crane the pupil in search of direction had found his ideal teacher.

INFLUENCE OF WILLIAM DEAN HOWELLS ON STEPHEN CRANE: THE REALISM WAR

As equally influential on the aspiring writer was William Dean Howells, to whom Crane sent a copy of *Maggie: A Girl of the Streets* in early March 1893. Shortly thereafter Howells invited Crane to his home to say how impressed he was with the novel and encouraged him to write realistically and to continue exploring the city in fiction. After interviewing Howells in October 1894, Crane wrote an article, "Howells Fears the Realists Must Wait," that clearly articulated what had become of the Realism War in American literature. Although Garland and Howells were encouraging fledgling writers to write realistically, a large section of the reading public was enamored of another kind of novel: sentimental love stories with dashing heroes and heroines often involved in melodramatic adventures. By the time that the interview occurred, writing these kinds of novels was a sure way to make a living, as attested to by the immensely popular George Du Maurier's *Trilby* and Anthony Hope's *The Prisoner of Zenda.*

The most successful American author—and the major spokesperson for the legitimacy of adventurous love stories—was the novelist, historian, and literary critic F. Marion Crawford. Crawford believed that an author should not be expected to deal with common people, probable events, and real-life issues, because the purpose of fiction was to amuse and entertain readers. Several titles of his more than 40 novels make his aim clear: *A Cigarette-Maker's Romance* (1890) is a love story about a Russian count and a poor Polish girl in Munich, Germany; *Khaled: A Tale of Arabia* (1891) is a love story about a genie seeking a soul mate; and *The Witch of Prague: A Fantastical Tale* (1891) combines the Gothic, the occult, and pseudoscience.

Crawford clearly articulated a justification for romance in *The Novel: What It Is* (1893).[2] "So far as supply and demand are concerned," he asserted, "books in general and works of fiction in particular are commodities and subject to the same laws, statutory and traditional, as other articles of manufacture" (12). Crawford distinguished romantic fiction, designed "to amuse and interest the reader," from the "odious thing[,] a 'purpose-novel,'" written by realists (11). Because a "novel is a marketable commodity," there is an "unwritten contract tacitly existing between writer and reader" (8, 12) concerning the purchase of fiction. Assuming that a novel is an "intellectual artistic luxury," readers feel cheated if they inadvertently buy realistic fiction, which is "an 'intellectual moral lesson'": "A man buys what purports to be a work of fiction, a romance, a novel, a story of adventure, pays his money, takes his book home, prepares to enjoy it at his ease, and discovers that he has paid a dollar for somebody's views on socialism, religion, or the divorce laws" (12, 13).

Howells's literary position, as articulated in the 1894 interview, can be read as a response to Crawford's 1893 book. The interview focuses on the battle in the literary marketplace between realistic and romantic fiction. Crane asked Howells whether or not he had recently "observed a change in the literary pulse of the country. . . . Last winter, for instance, it seemed that realism was almost about to capture things, but then recently I have thought that I saw coming a sort of a counter-wave, a flood of the other—a reaction, in fact." The counter-wave of romantic novels was unrealistic, Howells argued, because they lacked proportion and perspective and they equated life with "[l]ove and courtship": "Life began when the hero saw a certain girl, and it ended abruptly when he married her." A realistic novel, however, keeps love in perspective and sees it as simply one of "these things that we live in continually" (*Prose* 617). The most influential American critic of romance, Howells had already depicted the stereotypical romance novel as *Tears, Idle Tears* and "slop, silly slop" in *The Rise of Silas Lapham* and later coined an expression, *romanticistic novel,* to characterize a genre that "professes like the real novel to portray actual life, but it does this with an excess of drawing and coloring which are false to nature. . . . and endeavors to hide in a cloud of incident the deformity and artificiality of its creations" (Howells, *Literary Criticism* 218).

Recognizing the potential loss of income by ignoring popular taste, Crane speculated in the interview whether or not realistic novels would be "a profitable investment" if readers preferred romance to the accurate portrayal of common daily life. If fiction is a commodity to be bought by a publisher and sold to a consumer, then one's stock is bullish or bearish on the literary stock market depending on public acceptance. Though Howells encouraged a realistic writer to remain "true to his conscience," he acknowledged that the battle between private vision and public demand would be "a long serious conflict." Because the fate of American fiction was partly being decided by popular taste, realists faced a dilemma: Should they strive for an honest interpretation of reality, or should they simply cater to public demand for romance and become, as Howells called them, "public fools" acting like a "trained bear" in a circus or sideshow (*Prose* 616)?

As a child, Crane learned about the dangers of romantic stories from his father. In *Popular Amusements* (1869), a book criticizing amusements like idle reading, Rev. Crane sounded much like Howells: "novel-readers spend many a precious hour in dreaming out clumsy little romances of their own, in which they themselves are the beautiful ladies and the gallant gentlemen who achieve impossibilities, suffer unutterable woe for a season, and at last anchor in a boundless ocean of connubial bliss. . . . It is a vice of novelists as a class, to exalt love and matrimony above all else, and thus create in susceptible youth the habit of thinking and dreaming of matrimony above all else" (136, 142). Long before meeting Howells, Crane knew about the falseness of romance and chose early in his career not to be a trained bear in his pursuit of the profession of authorship. Describing his quest for Realism as "more of a battle than a journey," he wrote in spring 1894,

> I developed all alone a little creed of art which I thought was a good one. Later I discovered that my creed was identical with the one of Howells and Garland and in this way I became involved in the beautiful war between those who say that art is man's substitute for nature and we are the most successful in art when we approach the nearest to nature and truth, and those who say—well, I don't know what they say. They don't, they can't say much but they fight villianously [sic] and keep Garland and I out of the big magazines. Howells, of course, is too powerful for them.
>
> If I had kept to my clever Rudyard-Kipling style, the road might have been shorter but, ah, it wouldn't be the true road. . . . And now I am almost at the end of it. (*Correspondence* 63)

Even though the road to financial success "might have been shorter" by following such guides as Kipling, Crane had "renounced the clever school in literature" and chosen the road less traveled to remain committed to his quest for truthfulness in literary representation. "[T]he nearer a writer gets to life," Crane later concluded, "the greater he becomes as an artist, and most of my prose writings have been toward the goal partially described by that misunderstood and abused word, realism" (232). Crane's pursuit of authorship, however, was periodically frustrated by publishers. In 1893 when no one would publish his first book, *Maggie,* he printed it privately at his own expense; in 1894 negotiations over the publication of *The Black Riders and Other Lines* temporarily stalled because Crane and the publisher disagreed "on a multitude of points" (73); and in the same year he became convinced that S. S. McClure, who had held the manuscript of *The Red Badge of Courage* for six months without taking action, was a "Beast" who had kept him "near mad" and "in one of the ditches" of poverty (73, 79). By the time of the interview with Howells in October 1894, professional setbacks had certainly stretched Crane's patience, and although he was only two months away from national recognition with the newspaper publication of *The Red Badge,* he was still a year away from commercial success and international acclaim with the book publication of his war novel. Appropriately, as Crane fictionalized his own professional struggles in *The Third Violet* in fall 1895, he had initially titled it "The Eternal Patience."

Crane saw Garland and Howells less frequently in the last five years of his life because of his travels and outgrew their influence as he developed a technique more akin to Impressionism and Modernism, literary movements that moved Realism and Naturalism into new directions in American literature. Nevertheless, he never forgot his debt to his "literary fathers" and requested in his will that they be two of his literary executors (62, 265). Crane dedicated his first book of poetry, *The Black Riders and Other Lines* (1895), to Garland and thanked Howells in an inscribed copy of *The Red Badge of Courage,* which he unfortunately never received, for the "many things he [had] learned of the common man and, above all, for a certain re-adjustment of his point of view victoriously concluded some time in 1892" (247). The rest of this book will explore the impact of this readjustment.

NOTES

1. Standard time is a system that divides the world into 24 time zones. The difference in time from one zone to the next is one hour. Before the United States adopted the system in 1883, each city kept its own local time. As a result, trains leaving two different cities and traveling to the same city occasionally ran on different times.

2. Unlike Hawthorne, Crawford was using the word *romance* in its popular sense to refer to a love story often containing sentimentality, melodrama, and adventure.

3

Early Work

JUVENILIA

Crane's earliest surviving pieces of writing are a little-known poem and short story. The poem, written when he had just turned eight, is remarkable for its rhythm, humor, and irony:

I'd Rather Have—

Last Christmas they gave me a sweater,
And a nice warm suit of wool,
But I'd rather be cold and have a dog,
To watch when I come from school.
Father gave me a bicycle,
But that isn't much of a treat,
Unless you have a dog at your heels
Racing away down the street.
They bought me a camping outfit,
But a bonfire by a log
Is all the outfit I would ask,
If I only had a dog.
They seem to think a little dog

Is a killer of all earth's joys;
But oh, that "pesky little dog"
Means hours of joy to the boys.

(*Works* 10: frontispiece, 73)

Crane's penchant for irony and his love of dogs would remain with him throughout his life. The poem is also significant as evidence that Crane was literate by the age of eight. Although some biographers have incorrectly stated that Stephen did not attend school or learn to read until he was eight, by the time he had written this poem, he had been in school for about two years and had been on the honor roll.

His earliest known piece of prose, written when he was 13 or 14, is "Uncle Jake and the Bell-Handle." Uncle Jake and his niece are naïve country folk who come to the city to sell turnips and buy farm supplies. Despite Uncle Jake's belief in his level of sophistication, they constantly get taken advantage of. At the same time that he pulls on a bell handle, "a waiter of the hotel made a terrific onslaught on a gong that was sure to make any horses in the vicinity run away and awaken all the late sleepers for blocks around." Thinking he has mistakenly sounded an alarm that has "called out the fire department, or the police force or the ambulance corps or something else that's awful!" he fears he has become "a fergitive from justice, a critir hounded by the dogs of the law!" (*Works* 8: 3-7). Terrified, Uncle Jake and his niece abruptly leave town. Like his first poem, this piece is the work of an obviously precocious adolescent whose focus on irony, self-deception, and appearance versus reality foreshadows elements in his mature work.

SULLIVAN COUNTY TALES AND SKETCHES

Crane's first major venture into prose fiction grew out of camping trips near Port Jervis in Sullivan County, New York, that Crane and three of his friends took mostly in the summer of 1891. The experience led to a series of Sullivan County stories that feature the bizarre experiences of four men from the city while hunting, fishing, and camping. Though they are generally identified only by epithets—the little man, the pudgy man, the tall man, and the quiet man—they represent the four friends, with Crane being the quiet man (though Crane, at approximately 5' 7" in height, sometimes identifies with the little man as well).

Because the Sullivan County stories have been variously labeled as tales and sketches, there has been some debate about what specifically to call them. Cora Crane first used the title "Sullivan County Sketches" as the heading for two pieces in the table of contents of *Last Words* (1902), a misleading title for the book because it contains items written by Crane early and late in his career. In 1949 Melvin Schoberlin published 10 of the stories as *The Sullivan County Sketches of Stephen Crane,* and in 1968 R. W. Stallman, in *Stephen Crane: Sullivan County Tales and Sketches,* and Thomas Gullason, in "A Stephen Crane Find: Nine Newspaper Sketches," proposed expanding the canon. The problem of what to call the stories is the result of a matter of definition and technique. A "sketch" is often thought of as a brief composition focusing on a single scene or incident with little, if any, development of character or plot; like an artist's sketch, it can be used as a rough draft for a more finished product. A "tale" is typically a short narrative with the possibility of simple development, but like "sketch" it has been defined in various ways. One can merely think of the titles of Dickens's elaborate novel, *A Tale of Two Cities,* or Washington Irving's collection of essays and tales, *The Sketch Book.*

In addition, Crane complicated the distinction by calling at least some of the pieces "little grotesque tales" and by blurring lines between fact and fiction as he incorporates folklore and legend into his narrative. In "Not Much of a Hero," for example, he juxtaposes three contradictory interpretations of the life of a famous Indian fighter to raise questions about the nature of biographical evidence; and in "Sullivan County Bears," which describes the living and feeding habits of local bears as well as the hunting of them, the narrator comments that "it is difficult to reconcile the bear of fiction with the bear of reality" (*Works* 8: 219). In "The Way in Sullivan County: A Study in the Evolution of the Hunting Yarn," the narrator consciously draws attention to himself as an artist and as an interpreter of tall tales recounted to him by local residents: he is "the unoffending city man" who "seizes his pen and with flashing eye and trembling, eager fingers, writes those brief but lurid sketches which fascinate and charm the reading public while the virtuous bushwhacker, whittling a stick near by, smiles in his own calm and sweet fashion" (220-21). But even though he is aware of the obvious exaggeration in the tales recited to him as fact, he is not bothered by it: "In a shooting country, no man should tell just exactly what he did. He should tell what he would have liked to do or what he expected to do, just as if he accomplished it" (221). Viewed differently, the statement is a commentary on the creative process in fiction. A simple reporting of facts does not create meaning or have significance. Only through the recollection of facts that have been shaped imaginatively does one get to some sort of truth. Given these observations, it is not surprising that labels such as *story*, *sketch*, and *tale* are slippery when one attempts to categorize all of the Sullivan County pieces. Indeed, labeling Crane's artistry will be a constant problem throughout his career, as he will be called an impressionist, a realist, a naturalist, and a romantic at various times.

These "little grotesque tales of the woods which I wrote when I was clever" (*Correspondence* 111), as Crane characterized the Sullivan County stories, often rely on slapstick, tall tales, or the macabre to achieve an effect. The stories have a bizarre quality, as suggested by titles like "A Ghoul's Accountant" and "An Explosion of Seven Babies." In "Four Men in a Cave," for example, the little man boasts to his friends that they should explore a cave so that "'[w]e can tell a great tale when we get back to the city ...'" (*Works* 8: 225). Shortly after entering the cave, they lose their balance and their torches, tumble down the cave, and end up in a chamber, where they see a stone altar, candles in tin cups suspended from the ceiling, and a long-bearded, rustically dressed hermit holding a deck of cards. As they wonder if he is a "vampire," a "ghoul," a "Druid before the sacrifice," or the "shade of an Aztec witch doctor," he proclaims, "It's your ante" (228). Terrified, the little man plays poker with the hermit, who, never having won before, ironically wins all of the little man's money. The hermit then orders him and his friends to leave the cave. Later they learn that the hermit was a lunatic who had lost his wife and everything else because of compulsive gambling. In "The Mesmeric Mountain," the little man explores "an irregular black opening" into the forest because "it leads to something great" (268, 269). When he gets lost, he climbs a tree and sees a mountain. Though he decides to walk away from the mountain to get out of the forest, he somehow ends up at the foot of the mountain, which, with glaring eyes, seems to be coming toward him. As he runs away, the mountain seemingly follows him. Infuriated, he throws pebbles at it: "The little man then made an attack. He climbed with hands and feet, wildly. Brambles forced him back and stones slid from beneath his feet. The peak swayed and tottered and was ever about to smite with a granite arm. The summit was a blaze of red wrath" (271). After struggling to the top, he "swagger[s] with valor" because he believes he has defeated the mountain, but the narrator informs the reader of the truth: "The mountain under his feet was motionless" (271). In both stories a puffed-up ego gets deflated.

Though Crane later "renounced the clever school in literature" so that he could develop "a little creed of art" that "was identical with the one of Howells and Garland" (*Correspondence* 63) and that strove for truth in fiction, the Sullivan County tales and sketches foreshadow Crane's later treatment of irony, nature, and self-delusion. One need merely think of Henry Fleming's arrogance in *The Red Badge of Courage,* the harrowing experience of four men struggling to survive in the ocean in "The Open Boat," or the irony that exists in practically every story he wrote to realize that Crane was developing his major themes in these stories. As James B. Colvert notes regarding "The Mesmeric Mountain,"

> The relation of the fable to *The Red Badge* is obvious. It is at once a summary of the plot of the novel and an expansion of the metaphor by which Henry interprets his victory. There are the familiar elements—the terror and rage of the hero, the hallucinatory imagery, the antagonism of Nature, the delusive victory, the heroics, the narrator's ironic commentary.... The meaning of the fable is amplified elsewhere in Crane's fiction. The Swede in "The Blue Hotel," his mind swarming with terror at the threat of an unknown menace is, we discover, really at war with himself and an angry Nature.... And again we find the symbols of the fable in "The Open Boat," the story of the correspondent's anguished speculation about the meaning of an ambivalent Nature. ("Magic Mountain" 100–01, 104)

EARLY JOURNALISM

Besides writing fiction, Crane was also learning his trade as a journalist. He wrote for the school magazine of Claverack College and Hudson River Institute, which he attended from 1888 to 1890. During the summer months between 1888 and 1892, he worked for his brother (Jonathan) Townley, who had a summer news agency for the *New York Tribune* and the Associated Press in Asbury Park, New Jersey. Crane gathered society gossip and reported local events along the New Jersey coast.

During summer 1892 a distinguishing trait of Crane's shore reporting for the *Tribune* was an increasingly satirical look at pretension, arrogance, and moral smugness. In "On the Boardwalk" Crane satirized the middle-class visitor to Asbury Park "with a good watch-chain and a business suit of clothes, a wife and about three children"; the "summer girl," who "has been enshrined in sentimental rhyme and satirical prose for so long that it is difficult for one to tell just what she is and what she isn't"; and especially James A. Bradley, Asbury Park's mayor and principal property owner, who imposed his puritanical restrictions on dress and behavior on the town. He enforced Sabbath closing laws, confiscated the title deed of property if liquor was sold there, and constantly posted signs with priggish maxims, as in "Modesty of apparel is as becoming to a lady in a bathing suit as to a lady in silks and satins." As Crane quipped, visitors and residents "have signs confronting them at all points, under their feet, over their heads and before their noses. 'Thou shalt not' do this, nor that, nor the other" (*Works* 8: 516–17, 519).

More restrictive than Asbury Park was nearby Ocean Grove, a summer Methodist camp. As described by Townley,

> The by-laws absolutely prohibit dancing, card-playing or any such diversions as are prohibited by the general rules of the Methodist Episcopal Church, the buying and selling or drinking of spirituous liquors, excepting in cases of extreme necessity, and the sale of tobacco in any form. The strict observance of the Christian sabbath is rigidly insisted upon. The gates of the association are closed at midnight Saturdays and not opened until Monday morning at an early hour, excepting an inmate of the ground dies, when the undertaker is allowed to drive his wagon through the gates and remove the body to his warehouse. (*Log* 50)

Just as Stephen had found with the Asbury Park residents, those in Ocean Grove were ripe targets for his satire. As Methodist ministers arrived for a religious retreat and revival, he deflated the moral sternness of religious leaders who have reduced spirituality to a lifeless force: "[t]he sombre-hued gentlemen who congregate at this place in summer are arriving in solemn procession, with black valises in their hands and rebukes to frivolity in their eyes" (*Works* 8: 508).

Of all Crane's summer reporting, one article was to have far-reaching consequences for him. On August 17, 1892, the Junior Order of United American Mechanics (JOUAM) was scheduled to hold its annual American Day parade in Asbury Park. The primary goals of the JOUAM were "to restrict immigrations, and to protect the public schools of the United States and to prevent sectarian interference therein. We also demand that the Holy Bible be read in our public schools, not to teach sectarianism but to inculcate its teachings. We are bound together to promote Americans in business and shield them from the depressing effects of foreign competition. We are not a labor organization, nor are we a military company" (*Log* 78). Townley asked his brother to cover the parade for the news agency. Crane used the occasion to satirize the participants and observers of the event:

> The parade of the Junior Order of United American Mechanics here on Wednesday afternoon was a deeply impressive one to some persons.

There were hundreds of the members of the order, and they wound through the streets to the music of enough brass bands to make furious discords. It probably was the most awkward, ungainly, uncut and uncarved procession that ever raised clouds of dust on sun-beaten streets. Nevertheless, the spectacle of an Asbury park crowd confronting such an aggregation was an interesting sight to a few people.

Asbury Park creates nothing. It does not make; it merely amuses. There is a factory where nightshirts are manufactured, but it is some miles from town. This is a resort of wealth and leisure, of women and considerable wine. The throng along the line of march was composed of summer gowns, lace parasols, tennis trousers, straw hats and indifferent smiles. The procession was composed of men, bronzed, slope-shouldered, uncouth and begrimed with dust. Their clothes fitted them illy, for the most part, and they had no ideas of marching. They merely plodded along, not seeming quite to understand, stolid, unconcerned and, in a certain sense, dignified—a pace and a bearing emblematic of their lives. They smiled occasionally and from time to time greeted friends in the crowd on the sidewalk. Such an assemblage of the spraddle-legged men of the middle class, whose hands were bent and shoulders stooped from delving and constructing, had never appeared to an Asbury Park summer crowd, and the latter was vaguely amused.

The bona fide Asbury Parker is a man to whom a dollar, when held close to his eye, often shuts out any impression he may have had that other people possess rights. He is apt to consider that men and women, especially city men and women, were created to be mulcted by him. Hence the tan-colored, sun-beaten honesty in the faces of the members of the Junior Order of United American Mechanics is expected to have a very staggering effect upon them. The visitors were men who possessed principles. (*Works* 8: 521-22)

For Crane, who admired the precision of a military drill, the sight of marchers who "merely plodded along" was embarrassing. Crane was more critical, though, of greedy local residents, who viewed Asbury Park visitors as simply a way to make more money, and indifferent parade observers, whose "summer gowns, lace parasols, tennis trousers, [and] straw hats" revealed that they attended the parade simply to be seen.

When the JOUAM protested, the *New York Tribune* quickly printed a formal apology because of the biting criticism in the article and at least partly because the owner of the newspaper, Whitelaw Reid, was campaigning as the Republican vice-presidential nominee in a close 1892 election. In all likelihood, the *Tribune* feared offending voters. Local newspapers also covered the incident. As the

Asbury Park Journal reported, "This young man [i.e., Crane] has a hankering for razzle-dazzle style, and has a great future before him if, like the good, he fails to die young. He thought it smart to sneer at the Juniors for their personal appearance and marching, and the 'copy' editor of the *Tribune* made the same sad mistake. The article was in bad taste, unworthy a reputable reporter, and still more discreditable to a newspaper with the standing of the *New York Tribune*" (*Log* 80). Although rumors later spread that the incident helped to defeat the Republicans in the election, it is unlikely that it did. Townley and Stephen were apparently fired from the *Tribune*, though Townley was rehired. Stephen's career with the *Tribune*, however, was finished. After 1892 he never published another item in it, and during the next several years reviewers in the newspaper routinely condemned his books. After he moved to New York City in fall 1892, he found it extremely difficult during the next two years to work as a journalist, and not until 1894, with the help of William Dean Howells and Hamlin Garland, would that change. During this time, he rethought his career and began to pursue another literary outlet, extended prose fiction—a seminal decision that would lead to *Maggie: A Girl of the Streets*, one of the great pieces of late nineteenth-century American literature.

4

Maggie: A Girl of the Streets (1893, 1896)

1893 *MAGGIE*

Stephen Crane's first significant pieces of writing grew out of his experience in New York City. Undoubtedly, the most important is *Maggie: A Girl of the Streets (A Story of New York)* (1893, revised 1896), a groundbreaking novella in American literary Naturalism that John Berryman has said "initiated modern American writing" (52). Its depiction of a hostile, amoral universe indifferent to the plight of its inhabitants foreshadows the direction of much literary writing in America in the twentieth century. It is unclear, however, what influenced Crane to write a brutal account of urban slums. Before 1893 his literary output had consisted primarily of ephemeral journalistic pieces and the Sullivan County stories. Crane could have been influenced by the fictional and nonfictional treatments of tenement life in the late nineteenth century. The French novelist Émile Zola had earlier depicted a naturalistic universe in Parisian life in *L'Assomoir* and *Nana,* and Americans were developing a growing fascination with, and fear of, slum life in urban tenements, as reflected in such sociological studies as Rev. Thomas DeWitt Talmage's *The Night Side of City Life* (1878) and Jacob Riis's *How the Other Half Lives* (1890) and in the popularity of sentimental, melodramatic fiction like Albert W. Aiken's *The Detective's Ward; or the Fortunes of a Bowery Girl* (1871) and

Orphan Nell, the Orange Girl; or the Lost Heiress (1880). A dominant theme in the fiction, however, was rags to riches. In Edward Townsend's *A Daughter of the Tenements* (1895), for example, the heroine, despite the foils of a villain and her impoverished life selling fruit on the streets, becomes a successful ballerina, inherits a fortune, and lives happily ever after with her husband. When a slum novel lacked a happy ending—as with the seduction, betrayal, and death of the heroine in Edgar Fawcett's *The Evil That Men Do* (1889)—the ethical consequences of improper behavior were obvious.

Besides the uncertainty concerning the influences on *Maggie,* it is also unclear as to when Crane began writing it. Whereas several college friends at Syracuse University recalled seeing a draft of *Maggie* in spring 1891, other friends thought that he began writing it in 1892. Given Crane's fascination with the seamy side of urban life and his frequent trips to the Syracuse police courts to interview prostitutes, he most likely began a version of the novella while in Syracuse. The eventual subtitle of the novella reveals, though, that he ultimately thought of it as "A Story of New York."

Crane may have first envisioned the novella as a short sketch, "Where 'De Gang' Hears the Band Play," which was published in the *New York Herald* on July 5, 1891. Though the sketch was unsigned, newspapers at the time typically excluded the byline of unknown staff reporters. Nevertheless, certain characteristics about the sketch—the Bowery and Tompkins Square settings, the use of dialect and ethnic stereotypes, and the appearance of Jimmy and his sister, Maggie, who works in a factory—strongly suggest that Crane wrote it. If so, the sketch may represent an early version of the novella, which his Syracuse friends mistook as the longer *Maggie* in spring 1891. By the time Crane moved to New York City in fall 1892, he had either expanded the sketch into a longer manuscript or would soon do so. At this point he may have incorporated into the story additional geographical details that emphasize the New York setting, for example, references to the Brooklyn suburb of Williamsburg, the Central Park Menagerie, the Metropolitan Museum of Art, and Blackwell's Island, which he would have seen from his apartment overlooking the East River.

Because Crane could not interest a publisher in his novella, he used his own money and possibly a loan from his brother William to print the novella privately in New York sometime in late February or early March 1893 under the pseudonym "Johnston Smith." According to one of his friends, the pseudonym was meant as a joke; to another, Crane looked in the phone book for the two most common names and inserted a *t* into the first; to a third, the name "Johnston" was based on Crane's newspaper friend Willis Fletcher Johnson. The printer also chose to remain anonymous by excluding its name from the title page.

Given the subject matter, it is not surprising that Crane had trouble finding a publisher. Clearly missing from *Maggie: A Girl of the Streets* is the sentimentalizing or moralizing prevalent in other fictional treatments of tenement life in America in the late nineteenth century. Crane was not interested in analyzing the causes of, and offering solutions for, urban poverty. Although he may have been influenced by sociological tracts, sentimental fiction, or French Naturalism, *Maggie* is the first significant example of literary determinism in American literature. For Crane, who inscribed several copies of the novella, "it tries to show that environment is a tremendous thing in the world and frequently shapes lives regardless. If one proves that theory, one makes room in Heaven for all sorts of souls, notably an occasional street girl, who are not confidently expected to be there by many excellent people" (*Correspondence* 52, 53, 96).

In this environment, there is no escape from violence. As a child, Jimmie, "a tiny, insane demon," defends "the honor of Rum Alley" against "howling urchins from Devil's Row" (*Prose* 7); later, in his fight against Pete in a saloon, he is one of "three frothing creatures on the floor [who] buried themselves in a frenzy for blood" (50). Domestic life proves to be just as violent and chaotic. When Jimmie returns home after battling the "howling urchins," his mother "tossed him to a corner where he limply lay cursing and weeping" (11). Ongoing battles between the parents, "as if a battle were raging," are accompanied by "the crash of splintering furniture" (18). It is no wonder, then, that Maggie eats "like a small pursued tigress" and Jimmie comes home "with the caution of an invader of a panther den" (14, 18). Unlike sentimental fiction, Christianity offers no haven from this war-torn jungle. At best, it was ineffectual; at its worst, hypocritical. The poor woman who begs for money from the wealthy inhabitants of Fifth Avenue discovers that the "small sum in pennies" she receives "was contributed, for the most part, by persons who did not make their homes in that vicinity" (16). When Jimmie visits a "mission church" (20) to get a free bowl of soup, he is forced to listen to a preacher who condemns his listeners as sinners. It is ironic, then, that Maggie "blossomed in [this] mud puddle," grew up to be "a pretty girl," and seemed to have [n]one of the dirt of Rum Alley ... in her veins" (24). As she watches heroes rescue entrapped heroines in melodramas, she dreams of Pete as the "knight" and "beau ideal of a man" (28, 26) who will take her away from her bleak existence. Her mother, however, is jealous of Maggie's newly found happiness, and when Maggie tries to impress Pete by decorating the family apartment, her mother wrecks it in a drunken fury.

After Mary Johnson throws her daughter out of the home because she was "gettin' teh be a reg'lar devil" (29), Maggie turns to Pete for protection, but his interest in her deteriorates quickly, as depicted in the three music halls he takes her to in chapters 7, 12, and 14. The first one is a respectable place where families listen to an orchestra play "a popular waltz" (30). In the second one, however, a singer "in a dress of flaming scarlet" (52) performs a striptease as men pound tables with their beer glasses; and in the last one, with "twenty-eight tables and twenty-eight women and a crowd of men" (58), Pete deserts Maggie for another woman. Distressed, Maggie visits Pete at the saloon where he works, but her presence threatens his "respectability" (67). When she approaches a minister whose "eyes shone good-will," "he gave a convulsive movement and saved his respectability by a vigorous side-step. He did not risk it to save a soul. For how was he to know that there was a soul before him that needed saving?" (69). In a chapter in which the word *respectability* is used a half dozen times, Crane reiterates the importance of appearance to characters throughout the novella. When Jimmie is hitting Maggie in public, their father berates him to "[l]eave yer sister alone on the street" (12), implying that it is allowable to hit her at home where no one can see them; and when Maggie "goes teh deh bad, like a duck teh water," Mary Johnson laments, "Ah, who would t'ink such a bad girl could grow up in our fambly" (43). As with Pete, the minister, and the father, the mother's concern with appearance and respectability is steeped in hypocrisy.

Rejected by her family, Pete, and the church's representative, Maggie turns to prostitution for survival. In chapter 17, the most famous one in the novella, Crane compresses several months of Maggie's life as a prostitute into a single evening. As she walks from the theater district to the river, the imagery and her 10 potential clients depict her deterioration and eventual death. The "blurred radiance" of the "electric lights" and the "roar of conversation" of theatergoers are replaced by the end of the chapter with "a deathly black hue" of the river and a final "silence," as her clients range from the "tall young man" in "evening dress" to the "huge fat man in torn and greasy garments" (70, 72).

Though Crane is not explicit about whether the fat man kills Maggie or she commits suicide, there is clearly no hope for her. In the next chapter, Pete, the "aristocratic person" who had "loomed like a golden sun to Maggie," is reduced to a "damn fool" (26, 35, 78), and in a bitterly ironic conclusion to the story, Maggie's mother, upon learning of the death of her daughter, screams out, "Oh, yes, I'll fergive her! I'll fergive her!" (78). Although the novella emphasizes a Darwinian struggle for the survival of the fittest in a society in which family and church are meaningless institutions, Crane's use of irony throughout keeps the story from devolving into the pure Naturalism of Zola or the cheap melodrama of countless stories of innocent girls seduced and ruined by villains. Repeatedly, characters shield themselves from reality by creating hypocritical moral codes that supposedly pass as middle-class values.

Given Crane's unrelenting depiction of a brutal world, it is not surprising that the book went practically unnoticed. Crane later recalled that its lack of recognition was his "first great disappointment": "I remember how I looked forward to its publication, and pictured the sensation I thought it would make. It fell flat. Nobody seemed to notice it or care for it" (*Correspondence* 232). Although Crane sent out review copies and inscribed others to prominent people, only two reviews are known to have been printed in 1893, one in Crane's hometown newspaper, the *Port Jervis Union,* and one by his mentor Hamlin Garland in the crusading reform magazine, the *Arena.* Though Garland praised *Maggie* because "it voices the blind rebellion of Rum Alley and Devil's Row ... [and] creates the atmosphere of the jungles," he criticized its lack of "rounded completeness. It is only a fragment. It is typical only of the worst elements of the alley. The author should delineate the families living on the next street, who live lives of heroic purity and hopeless hardship" (Garland, "Ambitious French Novel" xi-xii). Similarly, John D. Barry, editor of *Forum* magazine, privately told Crane that though he did "really believe that the lesson of your story is good ... you have driven that lesson too hard. There must be moderation even in well-doing; excess of enthusiasm in reform is apt to be dangerous" (*Correspondence* 50). Compounding the problem with selling the book would have been its price of 50¢, a high price at a time when cheaply produced books in wrappers written by unknown authors were selling on newsstands for as little as 10¢. The only known copies sold were bought by a few of Crane's close friends at a party.

1896 *MAGGIE*

The fate of *Maggie* would change dramatically in three years. Following the book publication of *The Red Badge of Courage* in 1895 by D. Appleton & Company, Crane became an international celebrity.

Capitalizing on Crane's fame, Ripley Hitchcock, Appleton's literary advisor, wanted to republish Crane's novella and convinced Crane to revise it to eliminate objectionable passages. For several weeks in early 1896, as he wrote Hitchcock, Crane "dispensed with a goodly number of damns" and "the words which hurt" until "the book [wore] quite a new aspect from very slight omissions" (*Correspondence* 200). A collation of the 1893 and 1896 texts, however, reveals that the "very slight omissions" were actually more than 300 variants between the two versions. For example, the cursing and blasphemy in the 1893 version are deleted or replaced with such wording as "h—l," "d—n," and "gee." In another case in which Jimmie is encouraged to flee from battle with the "howling urchins from Devil's Row," he roars back, "dese micks can't make me run" (*Prose* 7). In the revised text Crane replaced the derogatory term for Irish immigrants *micks* with *mugs*. The numerous changes softened the language and made it less offensive. However, the major revisions by far occur in chapter 17, with the most important being the deletion of the penultimate paragraph, in which Maggie is followed by the fat, greasy man whose body "shook like that of a dead jelly fish":

> She went into the blackness of the final block. The shutters of the tall buildings were closed liked grim lips. The structures seemed to have eyes that looked over her, beyond her, at other things. Afar off the lights of the avenues glittered as if from an impossible distance. Street car bells jingled with a sound of merriment.
>
> When almost to the river the girl saw a great figure. On going forward she perceived it to be a huge fat man in torn and greasy garments. His grey hair straggled down over his forehead. His small, bleared eyes, sparkling from amidst great rolls of red fat, swept eagerly over the girl's upturned face. He laughed, his brown, disordered teeth gleaming under a grey, grizzled moustache from which beer-drops dripped. His whole body gently quivered and shook like that of a dead jelly fish. Chuckling and leering, he followed the girl of the crimson legions.
>
> At their feet the river appeared a deathly black hue. Some hidden factory sent up a yellow glare, that lit for a moment the waters lapping oilily against timbers. The varied sounds of life, made joyous by distance and seeming unapproachableness, came faintly and died away to a silence. (72)

The removal of the paragraph about the fat man eliminates the most graphic passage in the narrative, one that shows how desperate Maggie's plight as a prostitute has become. The imagery of death, jellyfish, and grease in the penultimate paragraph leads naturally into the final one, in which the "deathly black hue" of "waters lapping oilily" makes painfully clear that Maggie has died.

Crane found the process of revising the text exhausting. As he wrote Hitchcock, "The proofs make me ill. Let somebody go over them—if you think best—and watch for bad grammatical form & bad spelling. I am too jaded with Maggie to be able to see it" (*Correspondence* 224). The application of the Appleton house style, however, did more than just correct typographical errors and follow British orthography; in some cases it diluted meaning and tone.

Crane was anxious about Appleton's desire to make *Maggie* more marketable in order to profit from the success of *The Red Badge of Courage* because he feared that whatever he subsequently wrote would constantly be compared with "the damned 'Red Badge'" (127). "People may just as well discover now," he resigned himself to say, "that the high dramatic key of *The Red Badge* cannot be sustained" (191). Ironically, some critics disagreed with Crane's prediction. For William Dean Howells, whereas *The Red Badge* was confusing and repetitious, *Maggie* contained "that quality of fatal necessity which dominates Greek tragedy" (Weatherford 47). Similarly, a reviewer in the *Boston Beacon* praised Crane as "the first of American novelists to go into the slums of a great city with the intent of telling the truth and the whole truth, instead of seeking for humorous or romantic 'material'" (*Log* 188). Other reviewers, however, found it "an immature effort" (Weatherford 45) and "not true to life" (*Log* 216). At first, the book sold because of the popularity of Crane's war novel. In August 1896 the *Bookman* listed *Maggie* as fifth in book sales in the East and fourth in uptown New York, but the sales were short lived. No other later book of Crane's would make a best-seller list, and he would die in the shadow of "the accursed 'Red Badge.'"

CRITICISM

Much of the criticism of the novella focuses on the establishment of the text, its sources, its structure and imagery, and its relationship to Naturalism. The textual history of the two versions of *Maggie* remained unknown until the 1950s, when R. W. Stallman discovered that the 1893 and 1896 editions differed significantly ("Revision"). A decade later, while editing the complete works of Crane for a definitive, scholarly edition, Fredson Bowers made the controversial decision to conflate the two versions of *Maggie* and come up with a new version that

Bowers concluded was what Crane would have wanted had he not been pressured by his publisher to revise his text (*Works*, vol. 1). The problem with this approach, however, is that Bowers had to infer what Crane was thinking in 1893 and 1896. Though scholars have discounted this version—as do Hershel Parker and Brian Higgins in their textual analysis of Maggie's "last night" in chapter 17—Bowers's comments on this chapter, though at times forced, are still worth considering.

Marcus Cunliffe published a groundbreaking examination of possible European and American sources for the novella. Cunliffe paid special attention to the sermons of the well-known, controversial, American preacher Rev. Thomas DeWitt Talmadge, whose newspaper articles and extensive lecture tours promulgated the temperance movement throughout the country. Joseph X. Brennan has demonstrated how the ironic and symbolic structure of the novella reveals the self-righteousness of characters and their indifference to human suffering. Donald Pizer has argued that Crane "was less concerned with dramatizing a deterministic philosophy than in assailing those who apply a middle class morality to victims of amoral, uncontrollable forces in man and society" ("American Naturalism" 192). Possibly the best general examination is James B. Colvert's introduction to the Virginia edition of *Maggie*.

A major problem in the critical discussions of *Maggie*—indeed, one with much of Crane scholarship and criticism in the twentieth century—is that a number of the "facts" and legends about the novella have as their only source Thomas Beer's enormously influential, but apocryphal, biography *Stephen Crane: A Study in American Letters* (1923). The following assertions, for example, have no basis in fact: that Crane wrote the novella in two days before Christmas 1891; that his brother William gave the book its title and lent Crane $1,000 to print it; that Richard Watson Gilder, editor of *Century Magazine,* refused to publish it because it was "too honest"; that the printer was a publisher of medical and religious books and required Crane to sign a statement that he was 21; that the New York bookstore Brentano's sold only 2 copies and returned 10 to Crane; that a maid named Jennie Creegan used copies to start a fire; that a Catholic dignitary found it "an insult to the Irish"; and that Crane called the novella "a mud-puddle" in which he "tried to make plain that the root of Bowery life is a sort of cowardice" (81, 90, 86, 91, 94, 99, 140). Unfortunately, these assertions have been cited repeatedly in the criticism on *Maggie*. For an analysis of the damage done to Crane scholarship by Beer's fabricated biography, see Wertheim and Sorrentino ("Thomas Beer"), Clendenning ("Thomas Beer's" and "Biographers"), and Sorrentino ("Legacy").

A FEMINIST READING OF *MAGGIE: A GIRL OF THE STREETS*

Though critics use the expression *feminist criticism*, they define it differently. It does not mean that it refers to all the criticism written by women, for a male can be a feminist critic, nor does it mean that one cannot simultaneously be also, say, a Marxist critic. Generally, however, feminist critics would have the following interests: Because literary canons have been dominated by white males, feminist critics have been eager to discover the writings of women and people of color whose work should be part of the canon. This interest has also led to an awareness of why these writers were often discounted in a patriarchal society. Feminist critics have also been interested in exploring the extent to which gender differences affect the way one writes and reads literature. If there are significant differences between the ways that males and females use and understand language, they argue, then this affects the way one interprets literary texts. As a result of these differences, feminist critics are especially interested in how female characters are portrayed, often showing how they are oppressed politically, economically, and socially in a male-dominated culture.

Maggie: A Girl of the Streets exhibits the kind of oppression that women in cities faced in late nineteenth-century America. The economic opportunities were severely narrow. With the exception of those who might find work as a school teacher or nurse, most women were forced to perform menial tasks. With the invention of the first practical typewriter in 1867, the demand for secretaries increased, and with the development of manufacturing industries after the Civil War, women were needed to work on assembly lines. By far, the biggest demand was in the clothing industry, especially in shirt manufacturing. According to an 1889 report by the Department of Labor, women in shirt factories in New York City typically started at age 16, stayed on the job until they married, and made a little more than $300 a year (Campbell). Single women were expected to live with their families if they wanted to maintain their respectability. Consequently, employers shied away from hiring women who lived alone for fear that their presence might tarnish the image of the business.

Maggie certainly fits into this category. When she is old enough to work, presumably in her teens, her brother Jimmie says, "Mag, I'll tell yeh dis! See? Yeh've edder got teh go teh hell [revised to "go on d' toif" in the 1896 revision] or go teh work!": she can either become a prostitute or get a job. Like so many other girls of her age, "she got a position in an establishment where they made collars and cuffs. . . . [and a]t night she returned home to her mother" (*Prose* 24). She earned $5 a week, less than the weekly salary of a woman with an annual income of $300, and soon found the establishment "a dreary place of endless grinding" with "begrimed windows" and hot air that "strangled her" (28, 34).

After Maggie loses her job, gets thrown out of the house, and is rejected by Pete and the minister "whose eyes shone good-will" (69), she has no way of supporting herself except through prostitution. The general view in America in the nineteenth century was that women who became prostitutes did so because of moral weakness. Feminist critics, however, are interested in the validity of this assertion and would point to William W. Sanger's groundbreaking research on the subject. A medical doctor at the prison on Blackwell's Island in New York City, Sanger surveyed 2,000 prostitutes who were inmates there in the late 1850s and was surprised to discover the wide range of reasons that they gave for becoming prostitutes. A large number said they did so either because they had an "inclination" toward it or they wanted to avoid "[d]estitution" (488). The sense of moral failure was much lower on the list. Though there is no evidence that Crane read Sanger's *History of Prostitution* (1859), it was a standard reference text in the nineteenth century and was frequently reprinted.[1] There is no sense that Maggie feels bad about becoming a prostitute; she does it to support herself. Ultimately, Maggie dies not because she deserves to but because she is not strong enough emotionally to exist in a cruel universe.

Feminists would also be interested in Maggie's language—or more specifically her lack of it. In a story about her, she says practically nothing. Although other women, most notably her mother, speak their mind, Maggie has essentially been denied a voice. A passive character, she lives in a fantasy world wishing for her true love to rescue her from a dreary existence so that her life, like the plays she watches, will turn out happily ever after. She has implicitly accepted the subservient role that a patriarchal society has defined for women. Her value in this society is defined first by money earned on the job, then later as an object of sexual desire. Stripped of both alternatives, she has only one option: suicide. Not all prostitutes, however, end up tragically. Unlike Maggie, Nellie, another prostitute in the book, is a well-dressed "woman of brilliance and audacity" (*Prose* 59) who can manipulate men rather than be taken advantage of. Ironically, after

Pete abandons Maggie, Nellie steals his money, abandons the "damn fool" (76), and leaves him drunk in a saloon.

Feminist critics could argue that Crane's difficulty in publishing *Maggie* in 1893 is evidence of American society's inability to address social issues dealing with prostitution and the treatment of women as outcasts or second-class citizens. Even when Crane revised the book in 1896 to delete profanities, blasphemous epithets, and the depiction of Maggie's deterioration in chapter 17, the critical reception was mixed. Though the reading public was familiar with the character types in the novella—they were, as one reviewer noted, "old acquaintances" from the literature of "mean streets" (Cosgrove 13)—the dominant Victorian sensibility insisted that fiction about the slums have a strong moral basis and preach the virtues of home life and traditional Christianity.[2] Even if a prostitute were rescued from a life of vice and saved by religion, she could not expect that society would approve of her getting married. In *Maggie,* however, Crane does not moralize upon the ill effects of slum life; he exposes the hypocrisies of institutionalized Christianity, and he treats the shibboleths of society ironically. Not until Eugene O'Neill's *Anna Christie* (1921), in which a prostitute is forgiven and allowed to marry, will another American writer challenge as starkly as Crane a patriarchal society's attitudes toward women and sexuality.

NOTES

1. Interestingly, the narrator refers to Blackwell's Island, "the Island," at the beginning of *Maggie* (*Prose* 7).

2. This review has been erroneously cited as by Frank Norris. John O'Hara Cosgrove, editor of *The Wave,* is in all likelihood the author. See McElrath. The phrase *mean streets* is probably an allusion to Arthur Morrison's *Tales of Mean Streets* (1894), a collection of stories about slum life in London's East End.

5

Other New York City Stories and Sketches

GEORGE'S MOTHER

Following the completion of *Maggie,* Crane began writing a companion piece, *George's Mother,* in spring 1893, but he set it aside to work on *The Red Badge of Courage.* He returned to *George's Mother* in May 1894 and finished it in November. Thinking of the commercial failure of *Maggie,* however, he waited until after the success of *The Red Badge* before submitting it to a publisher. It appeared in 1896.

The novella depicts George Kelcey and his mother, who live in the same tenement house as Maggie Johnson's family. It soon becomes clear that George and his mother have a tense relationship. She constantly criticizes his behavior, tells him to get a job, and insists that he attend church with her. To some extent, her ongoing scolding of him is justified because he is lazy and immature and believes he should be treated "with reverence" by "men, and, more particularly, the women" (*Prose* 235). His "dream-woman, the goddess" is Maggie (237), but when she becomes attracted to Pete, George drowns his sorrow in a local saloon. Unfortunately, his group of drinking companions is as immature as he, and they create a drunken veneer of brotherhood to mask their own insecurities. His mother's attempt to help save him through religion fails. When he goes to church with her, "he felt a sudden quaking. His knees shook. . . . He felt completely alone and isolated at this formidable time" (255). Rather than being a source of moral strength, "the little chapel sat humbly between two towering apartment-houses," the light from "[a] red street-lamp" casting "the death-stain of a spirit" (255). From George's point of view, the image contrasts sharply with golden "brilliant lights" (255) uptown symbolizing life, but here—and throughout the story— George kids himself and sees only what he wants to see. When George gets into a fight with one of his friends at a party, the group rejects him. His situation quickly deteriorates as he loses his job and his money and joins a nihilistic gang of hoodlums, "all too clever to work," who "longed dimly for a time when they could run through decorous streets with crash and roar of war, an army of revenge for pleasures long possessed by others, a wild sweeping compensation for their years without crystal and gilt, women and wine. This thought slumbered in them, as the image of Rome might have lain small in the hearts of the barbarians" (262). But he even loses their support as he avoids a fight in order to see his dying mother. The story ends grotesquely as she screams and hallucinates, and he, staring at floral wallpaper, sees only "hideous crabs crawling on his brain" (276); in the background is the sound of a ticking clock on the mantel, a painful, inevitable reminder of the reality that ultimately destroys any attempt at self-deception. For both of them, romantic visions have devolved into hideous nightmares.

Contemporary reviewers recognized the power in *George's Mother*. One reviewer stated that Crane "knows that the essential thing in his line of work is to focus the vital facts in a given field of observation, without distortion; and this he succeeds in doing" (Weatherford 173); another reviewer pointed out the story's "bald realism"; and a third, despite disliking some of the prose style, praised it for being "a strong study of life among the poor of an American city" (175), though a fourth reviewer, apparently disliking local-color realism in general, dismissed the book as "simply an incoherent fragment told with no purpose and fraught with no interest." He believed that it was published to take advantage of Crane's sudden popularity after the appearance of *The Red Badge:* "We commend this precedent to Mr. Crane, and beg to suggest that an author who within a single year has forced critics to compare his work with that of the greatest living realists, ought not, as a mere matter of self-respect, to rake over his literary ash barrel and ask us to accept his old bones and junk as virgin gold" (177).

Unlike *Maggie, George's Mother* is less melodramatic in tone and less episodic in structure; instead, the action follows a tighter plot line, and the characters are developed with greater subtlety. There is also a hint that Mrs. Kelcey is modeled after Crane's own mother, who was vociferously dedicated to the efficacy of religion and to the Women's Christian Temperance Union (WCTU). Like Mrs. Crane, Mrs. Kelcey was traveling "aroun' th' country lecturin' before W.C.T.U's an' one thing an' another" (*Prose* 218). Both were strong-willed, pious women firmly dedicated to their beliefs. Similarly, George may be based on Stephen's brother Jonathan, who was an alcoholic. Stephen grew up constantly hearing from his mother about the dangers of alcohol and was familiar with his father's book about them, *Arts of Intoxification: The Aim and the Results* (1870). Unlike Mrs. Crane, however, Mrs. Kelcey is a blind fanatic who deludes herself into believing that George is a modern-day, altruistic monarch: "She rejoiced at qualities in him that indicated that he was going to become a white and looming king among men. From these she made pictures in which he appeared as a benign personage, blessed by the filled hands of the poor, one whose brain could hold massive thoughts and awe certain men about whom she had read" (235).

Like his mother, George romanticizes his own reality as a passionate melodrama:

> An indefinite woman was in all of Kelcey's dreams. As a matter of fact it was not he whom he pictured as wedding her. It was a vision of himself greater, finer, more terrible. It was himself as he expected to be. In scenes which he took mainly from pictures, this vision conducted a courtship, strutting, posing, and lying through a drama which was magnificent from glow of purple. In it he was icy, self-possessed; but she, the dream-girl, was consumed by wild, torrential passion. He went to the length of having her display it before the people. He saw them wonder at his tranquility. It amazed them infinitely to see him remain cold before the glory of this peerless woman's love. She was to him as beseeching for affection as a pet animal, but still he controlled appearances and none knew of his deep abiding love. Some day, at the critical romantic time, he was going to divulge it. In these long dreams there were accessories of castle-like houses, wide lands, servants, horses, clothes. (236)

Unwilling to accept the harsh truth that her son is an alcoholic, Mrs. Kelcey deludes herself into thinking

> in a vague way that he was a sufferer from a great internal disease. It was something no doubt that devoured the kidneys or quietly fed upon the lungs. Later she imagined a woman, wicked and fair, who had fascinated him and was turning his life into a bitter thing. Her mind created many wondrous influences that were swooping like green dragons at

him. They were changing him to a morose man, who suffered silently. She longed to discover them, that she might go bravely to the rescue of her heroic son. She knew that he, generous in his pain, would keep it from her. She racked her mind for knowledge. (232–33)

If George is the kingly leader of men who will protect his minions, Mrs. Kelcey is the knight who will protect him from the wicked influences of women and other evil "dragons." Life for her is an ongoing cosmic battle of good versus evil, whether she is defending her son against "green dragons" or simply cleaning house, "[h]er broom ... continually poised, lance-wise, at dust demons" (219). Both of them, however, suffer from the same problem: they choose to ignore who they really are and instead fabricate heroic illusions of themselves. As in *Maggie, George's Mother* depicts graphically the slums of lower Manhattan with their filth and decay and allows for the possibility that environment can affect human behavior, but he also criticizes those who hide behind romantic illusions and blame their plight on the environment.

NEW YORK CITY SKETCHES

Besides these two novellas, Crane wrote several memorable short sketches about Bowery life. Wanting to explore firsthand the Bowery in New York City, Crane spent a night in February 1894 with homeless men as they endured a blizzard that covered the city with almost 18 inches of snow. The experience led to "The Men in the Storm," which was published later in the year. Crane contrasts the homeless, huddled together in a line outside a 5¢ flophouse hoping to get in, with "scores of pedestrians and drivers ... scattering to an infinite variety of shelters, to places which the imagination made warm and familiar with the familiar colors of home" (*Prose* 577). The contrast between the haves and have-nots is further sharpened with an image of a financially secure businessman in his comfortable store across the street from the flophouse:

In the brilliantly-lighted space appeared the figure of a man. He was rather stout and very well clothed. His whiskers were fashioned charmingly after those of the Prince of Wales. He stood in an attitude of magnificent reflection. He slowly stroked his moustache with a certain grandeur of manner, and looked down at the snow-encrusted mob. From below, there was denoted a supreme complacence in him. It seemed that the sight operated inversely, and enabled him to more clearly regard his own environment, delightful relatively. (581)

Despite the obvious economic disparity depicted in the sketch, Crane had little interest in using literature didactically to create social change. Rather than telling readers what needed to be done to address the disparity, he was more interested in dramatizing the existing condition without moralizing upon it. Though the imagery of a violent snowstorm realistically re-created the weather at the time of the sketch, metaphorically the setting suggests that the social forces that create poverty or wealth are controlled by chance in a hostile, indifferent universe.

As with "The Men in the Storm," "An Experiment in Misery" was based on Crane's exploration of poverty in New York City. When this sketch was first printed in the *New York Press* in 1894, it was framed by an opening and closing passage that has not always appeared in reprints of the piece. In the beginning of the piece, the narrator and an older friend see a tramp and wonder how a poor person feels. Determined to find out, the narrator dresses up like a tramp so that he can conduct his experiment. At the end of the sketch, when the friend asks whether or not he has discovered the tramp's "'point of view,'" the narrator replies, "'I don't know that I did . . . but at any rate I think mine own has undergone a considerable alteration'" (1367). The deletion of the frame changes the narrative perspective from that of an outsider who observes a poor environment to someone who seems at least partly to be immersed in it.

The movement of the narrator is circular. He begins in City Hall Park and walks along Park Row, which at the time was the location for most of the major New York City newspapers. He continues to Chatham Square, the southern point of the Bowery (the skid row section of the city), then back to City Hall Park. During the first part of his journey, he enters a saloon that, like a monster with "ravenous lips," eats its customers as though they were "sacrifices to a heathenish superstition" (539). Looking for a place to sleep, he meets an "assassin" who takes him to a hellish, 7¢ flophouse where the human stench is "like malignant diseases with wings," a locker has "the ominous air of a tombstone," and a fellow occupant is a "corpse-like being": "With the curious lockers standing all about like tombstones, there was a strange effect of a graveyard where bodies were merely flung" (541, 542, 543). When another sleeping occupant wails during a nightmare, he expresses "the protest of the wretch who feels the touch of the imperturbable granite wheels, and who then cries with an impersonal eloquence, with a strength not from him, giving voice to the wail of a whole section, a class, a people" (543). However, the next day "the golden rays of the morning sun," like a knight battling a foe, "rout . . . the shadows" with "bright spears" and "a long lance-point," thus making the once death-like scene "commonplace and uninteresting" (544). Taking the assassin to breakfast, the narrator discovers that he blames his plight on a supposedly indifferent boss, a callous father, and blacks who will work for less money than whites. When they return to City Hall Park and sit on a bench, well-dressed businessmen pass them by without noticing them, which makes the narrator aware of "his infinite distance from all he valued. Social position, comfort, the pleasures of living were unconquerable kingdoms. He felt a sudden awe" (547). In conducting an experiment in misery, the narrator ultimately becomes aware of, and feels guilty about, the plight of the poor, but he does not sentimentalize their condition or suggest that they are simply powerless victims of an indifferent universe.

"An Experiment in Luxury," Crane's sequel to "An Experiment in Misery," appeared a week later in the same newspaper. As with the first piece, this one begins with a conversation between the narrator and his friend, who challenges a commonly held assumption that the rich have as many problems as the poor. To explore the assumption, the narrator accepts an invitation to dinner with a schoolmate and his wealthy family to investigate "[t]he eternal mystery of social condition" (552). Though the narrator is attracted to their opulent lifestyle, he views the family critically. The father is a dull man easily amused by the antics of a kitten, and his daughters seem interested only in the desire "to be beautiful" (539); however, the most devastating criticism is of the mother, who "was apparently not at all a dweller in thought lands" (554). A self-declared guardian of social proprieties, she has led "a life of terrible burden, of appalling responsibility" as she "scuffle[s] and scramble[s] for place before the white altars of social excellence" (554, 555). By the end of the sketch, the narrator's experience with his friend's family has led him to dismiss the false assumption "that riches did not bring happiness" and "that each wealthy man was inwardly a miserable wretch" (556). However, he does not seem interested in advocating immediate social changes and seems to believe that chance, not social or economic injustice, is the cause of the uneven distribution of resources in society.

Not as a stranger, therefore, did Crane write about the city's poor, for he often shared their condition. His empathy with social outcasts is evident in his depictions of experiences he shared with them, whether it be on a charity breadline or during a blizzardy night; but unlike many other writers at the time, Crane never theorized about the causes of social injustice, for he considered preaching "fatal to art in literature" (*Correspondence* 230).

6

The Red Badge of Courage (1895)

SOURCES AND INFLUENCES

The most famous novel about the American Civil War and the best dramatic depiction of it, *The Red Badge of Courage,* is Crane's masterpiece. Ironically, it was written by a youth who was born six years after the war had ended and who had never experienced combat firsthand. As a result, there has been much speculation concerning Crane's inspiration for the book. Some critics have suggested that he had read Russian and European war fiction—for example, Tolstoy's *Sebastopol,* Kipling's *The Light That Failed,* and Zola's *La Débâcle*—while others have argued that the influences were primarily homegrown, such as the scores of personal accounts, articles, and stories published in American newspapers and magazines throughout the latter part of the nineteenth century. One often-cited source is the series "Battles and Leaders of the Civil War," which was serialized in the *Century Magazine* from November 1884 to November 1887 and quickly reprinted as a four-volume set. Crane may also have interviewed veterans of the 124th New York State Volunteer Regiment, who first experienced combat at the Battle of Chancellorsville and who popularly were called the "Orange Blossoms" because they came from Orange County, New York. Situated in Crane's hometown of Port Jervis is a Civil War monument in Orange Square, where, as local legend has it, a young Crane talked with veterans.

If these veterans did influence the writing of *The Red Badge*, it would explain similarities between the 124th Regiment and Crane's fictional 304th. Although the book is primarily an internal narrative dramatizing Henry Fleming's constantly shifting emotional states, the external action, as Harold R. Hungerford has shown, is modeled partly on the Battle of Chancellorsville. For example, chapter 12, in which Henry receives his head wound, is based on the panic and devastating rout of the 11th Corps, which contained a number of Germans. Crane stereotypes them as "burly men" with a German accent who cry out, "'where de plank road? Where de plank road!'" (*Prose* 148), a question that refers to the Plank Road, which led to Chancellorsville. Though readers might momentarily wonder why Germans were fighting in the battle, Crane was accurate. The 11th Corps contained Germans; indeed, about a quarter of the Union troops overall were foreigners (Lonn 581–82). Likewise, the last chapter recounts the retreat of the Union forces toward the Rappahannock River. If the novel is based on the Battle of Chancellorsville, it would explain additional details. Both the 124th Regiment and the fictional 304th first saw combat during the Battle of Chancellorsville, and both had a private named Jim Conklin. After Chancellorsville, the 124th was transferred from the Third to the First Division of the Third Corps, and the men then wore the red diamond insignia, a red badge known as the "Kearny patch," devised by General Philip Kearny so that he could recognize the men under his command. Two of these patches that survive today bear the name of Private James Conklin (LaRocca).

Crane probably began writing *The Red Badge* in June 1893 and worked on it that summer at his brother Edmund's home in Lake View, New Jersey. In the fall he moved to New York City, finished the novel in April 1894, and gave it to S. S. McClure for publication through his syndicate or in *McClure's Magazine*, which featured personality profiles, fiction, and scientific news. When McClure kept the manuscript for six months without acting on it, an angry Crane wrote privately to Hamlin Garland:

> So much of my row with the world has to be silence and endurance that sometimes I wear the appearance of having forgotten my best friends, those to whom I am indebted for everything. As a matter of fact, I have just crawled out of the fifty-third ditch into which I have been cast and I now feel that I can write you a letter that wont [*sic*] make you ill. McClure was a Beast about the war-novel and that has been the thing that put me in one of the ditches. He kept it for six months until I was near mad. Oh, yes, he was going to use it but—Finally I took it to Bacheller's. (*Correspondence* 79)

Irving Bacheller, like McClure, had also set up a syndicate to supply newspapers and magazines with feature articles and fiction. Bacheller's recollection of meeting Crane and reading the manuscript is a memorable event in the publication of American literature:

> He brought with him a bundle of manuscript. He spoke of it modestly. There was in his words no touch of the hopeful enthusiasm with which I presume he had once regarded it. No doubt it had come back to him from the "satraps" of the great magazines. They had chilled his ardor, if he ever had any, over the immortal thing he had accomplished. This is about what he said:
> "Mr. Howells and Hamlin Garland have read this stuff and they think it's good. I wish you'd read it and whether you wish to use the story or not, I'd be glad to have your frank opinion of it."
> The manuscript was a bit soiled from much handling. It had not been typed. It was in the clearly legible and rather handsome script of the author. I took it home with me that evening. My wife and I spent more than half the night reading it aloud to each other. We got far along in the story, thrilled by its power and vividness. In the morning I sent for Crane and made an arrangement with him to use about fifty thousand of his magic words as a serial. I had no place for a story of that length, but I decided to take the chance of putting it out in instalments far beyond the length of those permitted by my contracts. It was an experiment based on the hope that my judgment would swing my editors into line. They agreed with me. (Bacheller 277-78)

In early December Bacheller arranged for an abridged version of *The Red Badge* to be published in newspapers over six days. By the middle of the month, Crane had shown newspaper clippings of the abridged version to Ripley Hitchcock, literary advisor to D. Appleton & Company. Crane signed a contract with Appleton in February 1895 for the book publication of the complete novel, but it did not appear until September because Crane was traveling in the West and Mexico during the spring.

CONTEMPORARY RECEPTION

From the outset, *The Red Badge of Courage* has been the center of controversy. American and British reviewers argued over which country's readers first recognized Crane's genius in *The Red Badge*. It is true that American reviewers recognized the importance of the book. Anonymous reviewers for the *Philadelphia Press* and the *New York Times,* for example, praised the book's literary style, its psychological realism, and its ironic treatment of war—topics that today still remain the focus of critical attention. The book, however, became popular with English readers more quickly, and English reviewers were generally more incisive in their comments. Two of the most important were George Wyndham's review in the *New Review* (London) and an unsigned review in the *Saturday Review* (London) in all likelihood by Sydney Brooks. With a greater awareness of Russian, French, and English literature than that possessed by American critics, Brooks considered Crane equal—in some cases, superior—to Tolstoy, Zola, Mérimée, and Kipling in depicting "the psychology of war—how the sights and sounds, the terrible details of the drama of battle, affect the senses and the soul of man" (Weatherford 101).

Wyndham, the most perceptive critic of *The Red Badge* during Crane's life, was an army veteran, politician, and literary scholar whose review is still one of the best introductions to the book. Wyndham distinguished between war accounts written by "gallant soldiers" interested "in strategy and tactics, not the universal curiosity of Man the potential Combatant." "[T]hey scarcely attempt the recreation of intense moments by the revelation of their imprint on the minds that endured them" (107). To understand these moments, "you must turn from the Soldier to the Artist, who is trained both to see and tell, or inspired, even without seeing, to divine what things have been and must be." More than any other contemporary critic, Wyndham anticipated what would be a major focus in criticism of the book in the twentieth century: Henry's point of view. According to Wyndham, "in all [Crane's] descriptions and all his reports he confines himself only to such things as that youth heard and saw, and, of these, only to such as influenced his emotions" (110).

Along with Wyndham's review, that by the American author Harold Frederic, at the time London editor of the *New York Times,* helped to draw British attention to Crane. Besides comparing Crane with other great nineteenth-century novelists, Frederic recognized the young author's remarkable originality in terms of point of view and treatment of reality and examined perhaps more thoroughly than any other reviewer of *The Red Badge* a central question: Can a writer who has never experienced war depict it more vividly than someone who has? After Crane moved to England, the two writers became close friends.

Despite widespread praise bestowed upon the novel in England and America, it was criticized, most notably in the American magazine the *Dial.* The associate editor, William Morton Payne, stated the official position of the *Dial,* and its owner, Civil War veteran General

Alexander C. McClurg, expanded upon the review by denouncing the book as "a vicious satire upon American soldiers and American armies" (140). Incorrectly assuming that it had first been published in England, he believed that it was an English attempt to embarrass American soldiers by dismissing them as either cowardly or ineffectual. The response supporting and criticizing him was immediate. Whereas J. L. Onderdonk, a newspaper editor from Idaho, agreed with General McClurg and dismissed the book as a "literary absurdity" (142), Ripley Hitchcock, the Appleton editor who arranged for the book publication of *The Red Badge,* presented facts concerning its publication and cited favorable reviews, and Sydney Brooks criticized McClurg for his "misjudged patriotism and bad criticism" (147). Given the widespread discussion about the book, it is not surprising that it was a best-seller in its first year of publication.

ANALYSIS

Though the novel treats war realistically, it is a psychological portrayal of a youthful recruit's terrifying experience of combat. Rather than focusing on external details such as weaponry, battlefield tactics, and other military issues, Crane was more concerned with the internal workings of the youth's ever-changing emotional state and attitude toward bravery and the nature of war. At the outset, the "youth," as he is called throughout much of the novel, is waiting to experience his first taste of combat. Because he had "dreamed of battles all his life," he expected war to be "a Greeklike struggle" like the kind in Homer's *Iliad* and the *Odyssey.* In his highly romanticized view of reality, he envisioned himself "in many struggles … with eagle-eyed prowess" (*Prose* 83). In contrast to his inflated sense of self is his mother's realistic response to news of his enlistments. Knitting his socks, packing his shirts, and giving him "a cup of blackberry jam" to take with him, she gives him motherly advice to stay out of trouble and to not think he "can lick the hull rebel army at the start" (85, 84).

Frustrated by the boredom of waiting for combat, he begins doubting his own view of war and questions whether he and his colleagues are heroes or cowards. Several unheroic incidents—for example, veterans who mockingly label new recruits "fresh fish," a soldier's accidentally stepping on a colleague's hand, and a "rather fat" soldier's trying to steal a horse from a "maiden" "with pink cheeks and shining eyes" (87, 95)—further confuse the youth about the nature of war. The youth soon thinks self-pityingly about his home life, recalling "the brindle cow and her mates" on the farm, and is willing to sacrifice "all the brass buttons on the continent to have been enabled to return to them." His situation worsens when the "loud soldier" speaks boastfully about his own self-confidence and "belief in success" on the verge of battle (90, 97). To the youth, "[n]o one seemed to be wrestling with such a terrific personal problem. He was a mental outcast" (98). Imagining himself the only coward in the army, "[i]n the darkness he saw visions of a thousand-tongued fear that would babble at his back and cause him to flee, while others were going coolly about their country's business" (98). He quickly finds out, however, that the loud soldier, with battle impending, becomes as scared as he does when the soldier gives him a "yellow envelope" with parting letters to his parents in case he dies (106).

As the 304th Regiment waits in a grove of trees to enter combat, another regiment quickly retreats past them—a "stampede" that is accompanied by "loud catcalls and bits of facetious advice concerning places of safety" from veterans and officers who "cursed like highwaymen," act like "a spoiled child," and gallop "about bawling" (109). Moments later the enemy attacks. Despite heavy casualties, the 304th stands ground, but when the enemy unexpectedly attacks a second time, the youth quickly flees. As he moves away from the battle, he overhears a conversation from which he learns that the 304th had held the line and not retreated. First feeling guilty because of his cowardice, he rationalizes the wisdom of his desire for self-preservation. When he throws a pine cone at a squirrel that runs away instinctively, he concludes that this is a sign from nature that all living things should avoid danger: "This landscape gave him assurance" (125). As he continues walking in the woods, "he reached a place where the high, arching boughs made a chapel. He softly pushed the green doors aside and entered. Pine needles were a gentle brown carpet. There was a religious half light" (126). Though the religious imagery and the calming aura of the setting suggest that he has found a safe haven, he is shocked by the horrifying appearance of a corpse, looking like "a dead fish" over whose "gray skin ran little ants ... trundling some sort of a bundle along the upper lip." Whereas nature seemed to be on his side only moments before, it now seemed to be hostile toward him, his body getting stuck in brambles and branches as he flees.

The youth eventually falls in with wounded soldiers struggling to get to the rear and wishes that he too "had a wound, a red badge of courage" (133). Two of the wounded are the "tattered soldier" and Henry's friend Jim Conklin, variously called the "tall soldier" or the "spectral soldier" (because his face is pasty gray). Suffering horribly, Jim wanders off to die, though with "a curious and profound dignity in the firm lines of his awful face" (137). Enraged by the cruelty of war, Henry shakes his fist at the battlefield as though "about to deliver a philippic" (137). The tattered soldier, however, suggests that they move on, especially because he is becoming increasingly weak from his wounds. Assuming that Henry must also have been wounded since he is not with his regiment fighting, he advises Henry, "Ye'd better take keer of yer hurt. It don't do t' let sech things go. It might be inside mostly, an' them plays thunder. Where is it located?" (139). Without knowing it, the tattered soldier is, of course, right, for Henry's wound is psychological. Unlike the soldiers he is marching with, he has been weakened not by a literal wound but by his own conflicting emotions about himself in regard to the war. Although the tattered soldier obviously needs comforting as he dies, Henry deserts him "wandering about helplessly in the field" (141).

Finding himself alone again, he struggles with his conflicting emotions. More so than many of the other chapters, chapter 11 takes place almost completely in Henry's mind as it records his rapid shifts between optimism and despair, self-glorification and self-denunciation, as well as romanticized views of self and realistic depictions of the effects of war. On the one hand, Henry imagines melodramatic images of himself as a heroic martyr valiantly leading on his troops: "Swift pictures of himself, apart, yet in himself, came to him—a blue desperate figure leading lurid charges with one knee forward and a broken blade high—a blue, determined figure standing before a crimson and steel assault, getting calmly killed on a high place before the eyes of all. He thought of the magnificent pathos of his dead body" (143). When he sees troops fleeing from battle, he feels comforted and not alone in his decision to run. If the North loses, he concludes, the defeat is "a round-about vindication of himself … that would prove, in a manner, that he had fled early because of his superior powers of perception" (145). But just as quickly as he can rationalize his behavior, he remains haunted with guilt. When he sees troops heading into battle, he feels depressed because "the sore badge of his dishonor" has made him "a craven loon" (146, 145). Unable to hide the truth from himself, he fears that others will immediately recognize his cowardice.

Within moments of advancing into battle, Union troops panic and run like "terrified buffaloes" (148). Horrified, Henry can only conclude that they have lost the fight. When he tries to question one of the fleeing men, Henry gets hit in the head with the butt end of a rifle. Ironically, what will become his own red badge of courage is the result not of direct combat but of the actions of a terrified Union soldier deserting just as Henry had done.[1] Dazed and confused, Henry wanders until a man with "a cheery voice," seeming to possess "a wand of a magic kind," leads him back to his regiment, "thread[ing] the mazes of the tangled forest with a strange fortune" (152, 153). Afterward, Henry realizes "he had not seen his face" (153).

Embarrassed, Henry returns to camp and is relieved to discover that Wilson, no longer the "loud soldier" but now a humble person called "the friend," is glad to see him. Like a caring mother, Wilson binds Henry's head wound, gives him coffee, and prepares his bedding. Feeling superior, however, Henry acts condescendingly toward his friend, especially when Wilson sheepishly asks for the return of his yellow packet of letters. Rather than acknowledging his own wartime fears, Henry sees the packet of letters as "a small weapon with which he could prostrate his comrade at the first signs of a cross-examination" about his own disappearance during combat (164). Because only he knows about "his mistakes in the dark," he rationalizes that "he [is] still a man" and thus has "license to be pompous and veteranlike" (165). As Henry has done throughout the novel, he fictionalizes the reality of his situation:

> After this incident, and as he reviewed the battle pictures he had seen, he felt quite competent to return home and make the hearts of the people glow with stories of war. He could see himself in a room of warm tints telling tales to listeners. He could exhibit laurels. They were insignificant; still, in a district where laurels were infrequent, they might shine.
>
> He saw his gaping audience picturing him as the central figure in blazing scenes. And he imagined the consternation and the ejaculations of his mother and the young lady at the seminary as they drank his recitals. Their vague feminine formula for beloved ones doing brave deeds on the field of battle without risk of life would be destroyed. (166)

For Henry, bravery in battle has less to do with personal duty, responsibility, and patriotism and more with sentimental adulation from others.

Soon, the 304th Regiment marches to relieve another regiment that has been in combat. Henry begins a harangue in which he complains about his commanding officers and his own plight, then blames the enemy for his problems. "[W]ith his eyes burning hatefully and his teeth set in a curlike snarl," he envisions the enemy as "flies sucking insolently at his blood," and when fighting begins, he acts like "a war devil" shooting wildly even after the enemy has retreated (172, 173, 175). Delighted by Henry's warlike spirit, the lieutenant says, "By heavens, if I had ten thousand wild cats like you I could tear th' stomach outa this war in less'n a week" (174–75). Ironically, just as his earlier flight from combat was instinctive, so too is his maniacal fighting, thus suggesting a tenuous line between cowardice and bravery. Curiously, the narrator comments on the nature of heroism itself: "There was the delirium that encounters despair and death, and is heedless and blind to the odds. It is a temporary but sublime absence of selfishness" (183). The actual act of bravery, it would seem, is not a reasoned, ethical choice but an unconscious act performed irrationally.

Despite the intense fighting by the 304th, the troops are criticized for not going an extra 100 feet. Henry, however, acts smugly and is further satisfied with his own behavior when he is commended for his bravery. When the next charge occurs, Henry carries the regiment's flag into combat, though he still views war romantically. The combat results in the capture of four enemy soldiers, each of whom symbolizes an aspect of Henry in the story. Whereas one has "a superficial wound," another is "a boy in years," a third is "morose," and a fourth is filled with "[s]hame" (207, 208). The composite image of a youthful soldier with turbulent emotions sets up the final chapter in which the reader must decide whether or not Henry has matured as a result of his experience.

In contrast to the first day of fighting, during which Henry fled out of fear, on the second day he seems to have resolved his doubts about his own ability to be part of a fighting machine. He fights courageously, helps lead troops into combat even though he has heard a general say that few will survive the ordeal, and carries the regiment flag even though doing so makes him an easy target. Examined closely, however, his "courage" is not the result of patriotism or a sense of duty to his comrades but the result of rage and fury: "He had a wild hate for the relentless foe. Yesterday, when he had imagined the universe to be against him, he had hated it, little gods and big gods; to-day he hated the army of the foe with the same great hatred" (172). His actions, whether running away from or into combat, are as instinctive as those of an animal. Ironically, in the eyes of his friends he has become a hero who has earned his "red badge of courage."

CRITICAL PERSPECTIVES ON CHARACTERIZATION

Whether or not Henry has indeed become a mature hero at the end of the story has been one of the most debated issues about the book. Given Henry's constant shifts between smug confidence and self-doubt, some critics find it difficult to accept that a youth could suddenly gain maturity after only two days. Stated more broadly, the question is this: By the end of the novel, should readers agree with Henry that he has grown in insight and has become a man; should they read the ending ironically, thus suggesting that Henry is as much the victim of his own romantic delusions as he was in chapter 1; or is the narrator—possibly even the author himself—ambivalent about Henry? The most famous argument that Henry matures from his experience has been presented by R. W. Stallman in his introduction to *The Red Badge*. According to Stallman, the key to the novel is the Christian symbolism, in which Jim Conklin's death is a reenactment of the death of Jesus Christ. Like Christ, Jim Conklin has the initials J. C., has a torn body, gory hand, and wound in his side; has "a resemblance in him to a devotee of a mad religion"; stirs in others "thoughts of a solemn ceremony"; and is spoken of as "Gawd! Jim Conklin!" (*Prose* 136, 133). When he dies, "[t]he red sun [that] was pasted in the sky like a wafer" (137) symbolizes the sacramental communion wafer. For Stallman, this redemption experience signifies the larger one for Henry, who undergoes a moral awakening that leads to his emotional growth; however, Stallman's religious interpretation to explain Henry's character has been much debated because much of the symbolism in the novel has nothing to do with Christianity. John F. Hart explains this symbolism in terms of a classic initiation story in mythology in which the hero, after facing physical and emotional trials, is reborn into a greater awareness of self. Hart points out numerous images—for example, a threatening monster, ominous landscape, entombment, food and drink, and a guide when one is lost—that appear repeatedly in initiation stories in which an isolated individual learns through experience how to be part of a larger good.

Other critics rely less on patterns of religious or mythological images to explain the text and have a more limited focus. A number of these critics—for example, James B. Colvert ("Structure and Theme"), Eric Solomon ("Structure"), and Marston LaFrance—believe that Henry gains some small amount of social and moral awareness as he moves from being an isolated individual to becoming a loyal and dutiful member of a group. Viewing this newly found awareness differently, James Trammell Cox and Robert Shulman see Henry's shifting from a romantic to a more naturalistic vision of reality as a hostile universe. Another group of critics, most notably Daniel Weiss, psychoanalyzes Henry's growth into maturity as an internal battle in which he defeats his fears and anxieties.

In contrast to critics who argue that Henry develops as a character are those who see no change in him and those who find ambivalence in the way that Crane treats him. For Stanley B. Greenfield Henry has learned something from his experience, though he still does not fully understand and is still prone to delusion. As the famed American novelist Ralph Ellison has written, "although Henry has been initiated into the battle of life, he has by no means finished with illusion—but that, too, is part of the human condition" (18). Other critics, however, find this ambivalence about whether or not Henry has been morally rejuvenated a weakness in the book. For Clark Griffith, who believes that irony is central to Crane's narrative techniques in many of his stories, Henry has learned little despite his attitude at the end of the novel. This, though, is to be expected when the meaning of life is undecipherable; consequently, humans rationalize a sense of moral growth as a defense against an indifferent universe. According to Griffith, Crane undermines a story seemingly about moral regeneration with an ambivalent ending. The noted American poet John Berryman put it more bluntly: "I do not know what Crane intended. Probably he intended to have his cake and eat it too—irony to the end, but heroism too" (90).

CRITICAL PERSPECTIVES ON IMAGERY, STRUCTURE, AND POINT OF VIEW

In addition to analyses of Henry's character and the composition of the text, critics have focused on formal characteristics of the book, for example, imagery, structure, and point of view. Even in a cursory reading of the novel, one cannot help noticing the constant mention of color, as though Crane were painting a picture with words, using color literally to describe what Henry sees and figuratively to depict how he feels. For example, uniforms are blue or gray, fire is red, sunlight is orange and yellow, and foliage is green. However, there are also "sorry blue" and "the gray seal of death" (*Prose* 118, 130). Whereas red can suggest the rage of "the red wings of war," "the green doors" of nature suggest a serene setting. When Henry speaks of his romantic illusions about warfare, his mother confronts him with the truth by deflating his dreams with a "yellow light thrown upon the color of his ambitions" (143, 126, 84). Crane was no stranger to art. His mother and an older sister were painters, and many of his friends while he worked on *The Red Badge* were painters and illustrators. One of the major aesthetic movements at the time was Impressionism, which stated that painters should try to recreate the sensory impression that color and light have on the eye. The focus was on the individual's subjective perception of reality rather than an attempt to recreate reality objectively. Applied to literature, this approach argues for a limited point of view rather than an omniscient author. Such is the case in *The Red Badge*. In the opening paragraph, before Henry's perspective is introduced, an unidentified third-person narrator records not so much what exists objectively but what his or her impressions are of the scene based on color and light:

> The cold passed reluctantly from the earth, and the retiring fogs revealed an army stretched out on the hills, resting. As the landscape changed from brown to green, the army awakened, and began to tremble with eagerness at the noise of rumors. It cast its eyes upon the roads, which were growing from long troughs of liquid mud to proper thoroughfares. A river, amber-tinted in the shadow of its banks, purled at the army's feet; and at night, when the stream had become of a sorrowful blackness, one could see across it the red, eyelike gleam of hostile camp-fires set in the low brows of distant hills. (81)

The scenery is not literally changing "from brown to green," but as morning approaches and the fog lifts, the impression one gets is of changing colors; nor is the scenery, like a person, actually "sorrowful" or "hostile," but one senses a feeling of something ominous and foreboding. The point of view shifts immediately to that of Henry, where it essentially stays until the last paragraph of the story, in which the unidentified narrator reappears. Throughout the book, the focus is on Henry's fragmented, disconnected experiences over two days. He knows little about what is objectively going on around him. Often what he hears are rumors, and when he tries to see clearly, he is stymied by darkness, smoke, and gunfire. Rather than having an omniscient narrator who sees the big picture and records accurately, readers are given subjective impressions of a raw recruit experiencing terror firsthand. As Sergio Perosa has argued,

> *The Red Badge of Courage* is indeed a triumph of impressionistic vision and impressionistic technique. Only a few episodes are described from the outside; Fleming's mind is seldom analyzed in an objective, omniscient way; very few incidents are extensively *told*. Practically every scene is filtered through Fleming's point of view and seen through his eyes. Everything is related to his *vision*, to his *sense*-perception of inci-

dents and details, to his *sense*-reactions rather than to his psychological impulses, to his confused sensations and individual impressions. (88)

As evidence of how extensive Henry's sensory impressions are, Perosa did "[a] simple statistical analysis on the linguistic level" of the novel:

> One is struck at first glance by the recurrence of terms indicating visual perceptions. Verbs like *to see, perceive, look, observe, gaze, witness, watch, stare, peer, cast eyes, discover,* etc. appear on practically every page, indeed, no less than 350 times in this fairly short novel. Expressions like *to seem, appear, look like, exhibit, glare, gleam, shine, flash, glimmer, display, loom, show, reveal,* etc. occur no less than 200 times. Less numerous, but still quite frequent, are verbs of auditory perceptions (like *to hear,* etc.) or those expressing inner feeling (*to feel,* etc.) especially when Henry Fleming is wounded or regaining consciousness. (88–89)

Given the overwhelming importance of sensory data to Henry, it is not surprising that "[a] thousand details of color and form surged in his mind" just before the enemy attacks (*Prose* 111). As much as any novel in American literature, *The Red Badge of Courage* is filled from the first to the last page with one person's immediate impressions of events as he experiences them.

THE RED BADGE OF COURAGE AND AMERICAN CULTURAL HISTORY

Whether or not one believes that these impressions are the basis for moral and emotional growth in Henry, the novel clearly reflects America's vast change in self-identity in the last part of the nineteenth century. Before the Civil War, America saw itself as largely simple, rural, and self-sufficient, appropriately symbolized by Henry's being a schoolboy who helps his mother on their farm and who "ain't never been away from home much" (*Prose* 85). Following the Civil War, however, the dream of an agrarian democracy confronted the reality of a society increasingly being forced to change because of the rise of big business, political corruption, and civil unrest. This was the period that saw the imprisonment of political leader "Boss" Tweed in 1873, the Haymarket Square Riot in 1886, and the stock market crash in 1893. Feeling themselves dehumanized by an increasingly technological society, farmers and laborers formed the Populist Party in 1891. The march of Coxey's Army, a group of several hundred unemployed workers, on Washington, D.C., prompted a number of other marches to protest the plight of the jobless in America. Thus, in *The Red Badge of Courage* when troops are "machines of steel," the roar of warfare is like "the whirring and thumping of gigantic machinery," and Henry feels trapped "in a moving box" forced to follow "iron laws of tradition and law on four sides" (119, 200, 101), he is experiencing the result of humanity's being seemingly reduced to nothing more than a machine. As Frederick C. Crews has noted,

> In a sense, therefore, *The Red Badge* is a faithful, though oblique, reflection of the era in which it was written; it expresses certain doubts about the meaning of individual virtue in a world that has become suddenly cruel and mechanical. For this very reason, however, Crane's novel fails to typify the literary tastes of the nineties. Most Americans still regarded literature as an amusing diversion from life rather than an honest image of it, and the most popular writers, such as Thomas Bailey Aldrich, Francis Marion Crawford, and James Whitcomb Riley, were usually the most socially innocuous. More serious novelists like [Henry] James and [William Dean] Howells strove to be realistic, but they did nothing to deny the prevailing belief that fiction should be refined, unsensational, and concerned with ethical ideals. The canons of genteel taste, formulated by such respected critics as George E. Woodberry, William C. Brownell, Edmund C. Stedman, and Charles Dudley Warner, demanded a lofty tone and a high moral purposefulness. *The Red Badge of Courage* does not simply fail to meet such expectations, it deliberately flouts them; and we may fix one element of Crane's relation to his times by saying that he self-consciously tried to break all the rules of the Genteel Tradition. (xii–xiii)

Crane's desire to break literary rules is certainly clear if one compares *The Red Badge of Courage* with other war fiction in the nineteenth century. Heavily influenced by Sir Walter Scott, novelists treated war as a romantic adventure involving patriotic heroes who fought chivalrously for honorable causes. The plots of the novel were melodramatic and often had a domestic love story. Although a few of Crane's contemporaries wrote realistically about war, none of them succeeds as successfully as Crane in capturing the intensity of combat and parodying romantic treatments of war. As Eric Solomon has shown, "*The Red Badge of Courage* employs previous assumptions about heroic soldiers that informed almost all popular Civil War fiction before the rise of realism in the 1890's in order to reject them" (*From Parody to Realism* 73). Rather than a natural-born hero, Henry Fleming is an unnamed youth for much of the novel who deserts, gets wounded in a most ironic way, and ends up being considered a hero by his comrades because of his "red badge of courage." To call attention to the customary love story in popular war fiction, Crane briefly alludes to a dark-haired girl who "grew demure and sad at sight of" Henry's departure for war but undercuts it with a "certain light-haired girl [who] had made vivacious fun at his martial spirit" (*Prose* 86); there will be no damsel in distress, no sentimental heroine, waiting for him upon his return from war. In short, *The Red Badge of Courage* challenged the "iron laws of tradition" on how to portray war. At the outset of the novel, when Henry says, in talking about the tall soldier's description of a rumored imminent battle, that "like as not this story'll turn out jest like them others did" (89), Crane is also alerting the reader to his own intention. In breaking literary laws of tradition, he had written a new kind of American war fiction that remains the touchstone against which other war novels have been judged. Ernest Hemingway believed that there was no "real literature of our Civil War" until *The Red Badge of Courage* (*Men at War* xvii); William Faulkner considered it "the only good war story I know" (Blotner 69); and F. Scott Fitzgerald, criticizing Hollywood for its unrealistic treatments of the Civil War, recommended that filmmakers read Crane's novel (Turnbull 597). Today, more than a hundred years after its first publication, *The Red Badge of Courage* captures as well as any other novel the frightening experience of combat.

A TEXTUAL READING OF *THE RED BADGE OF COURAGE*

Inexperienced readers often think that what they are reading on the page is what an author originally intended. As any writer knows, however, a written document—whether it be a piece of fiction, a term paper for school, or simply a list of daily tasks—undergoes revision as one rethinks the subject. It is not surprising to have multiple drafts of the same document. If one has written, say, a novel, the process of getting it published is complex. A literary editor at a publishing house might require the author to revise the manuscript again for all sorts of reasons, for example, it is too long, it does not appeal to popular taste, or it needs clarification of plot or character development. It is also quite possible that the author decides to make any number of changes on his or her own rather than being required to do so. If the novel was being serialized in a newspaper or magazine, as was sometimes the case in the nineteenth century, portions might be deleted so that the novel could fit into the designated number of newspaper columns or magazine pages. As the novel is being prepared for print, a typesetter might inadvertently set the wrong type and thus introduce changes into the text. If the novel was going to be published in, say, England, there would be additional considerations concerning American versus British usage and orthography. In short, a number of factors affect what text readers ultimately end up reading. An examination of these factors is the aim of textual criticism.

Textual critics have several tasks: First, they analyze the physical characteristics of an author's handwritten manuscript or typescript. They note, for example, the deletions and insertions of words and passages to record at least part of the author's thought process while composing. If the date of the composition is unknown, other characteristics—for example, the kind of paper used, the color of ink, or the size of handwriting—may help to establish when it was written. Second, textual critics want to examine the typescript that a publisher has prepared for publication to see if an author has decided to make last-minute revisions. Third, they want to establish a reliable text for readers that includes as best as possible the author's final intentions. Ideally, textual critics have all of the physical evidence available to them. Realistically, however, this is often not the case. Manuscripts and typescripts get lost or discarded, revisions in them may be hard to read, and other revisions may have been transmitted orally without any written record so that one does not know if they were made by the author or editor. One of the best examples in American literature of these issues is the publication history of *The Red Badge of Courage.*

The question of how to interpret Henry's character is complicated by the dramatic difference between the manuscript of the novel and the version published by Appleton in 1895. After completing a portion of the first draft, Crane started over. Lacking paper, he wrote on the blank sides of the first draft and eventually completed a novel of 25 chapters and about 55,000 words. When S. S. McClure hesitated to publish it, the Bacheller news syndicate published an abbreviated version of 18,000 words that appeared in newspapers in December 1894. The October 1895 Appleton book version, at a little more than 46,000 words, reinstated much of the text deleted in the newspaper version, but the book was still considerably shorter than the manuscript. As one might surmise, the differences are more than simply cosmetic. In the newspaper version, the story emphasizes external action over Henry's internal philosophical debates and ends with his clearly becoming a hero; in the manuscript version, Henry is as full of self-delusion at the end of the story as he was in the beginning; and in the book version, the story is more complex psychologically at the end to suggest that Henry, though not fully mature, has gained some limited knowledge from his experience. Because the newspaper version was designed simply as leisure reading for Sunday readers, it can in no way be considered an authoritative version of *The Red Badge of Courage*.

There is, however, much debate and confusion about the other two versions of the story. Among the revisions in the manuscript that appear in the book are changes in dialect; a change of many proper names to epithets like "the youth," "the loud soldier," and "the tall soldier"; and the deletion of a whole chapter and of long passages in other chapters. Changes in the manuscript are typically signified by crossed-out passages, but in other cases, passages in the manuscript not crossed out do not appear in the published version. Moreover, passages such as the last line of the book are not in the manuscript at all. Consequently, scholars have had to infer what happened between the inception of the book and its appearance. Did Crane make all of these revisions on his own, and if so, when? In spring 1894 Crane asked Hamlin Garland to read and comment upon the manuscript of *The Red Badge*. Garland penciled suggested corrections on the manuscript. What is uncertain is how many revisions Crane actually made at this time. Fredson Bowers (*Works* 10: 199–203), Donald Pizer ("*Red Badge*" 77–81), and James B. Colvert ("Crane, Hitchcock" 248–49) have argued that he removed the original chapter 12 from the manuscript and made the other extensive deletions at the conclusions of chapters 7, 10, and the original chapter 15 containing Henry Fleming's interior monologues rationalizing his cowardice and rebellions against the universal order in spring 1894. Henry Binder (11–23, 42 n. 7) and Hershel Parker (35–41), however, have argued that the Appleton editor Ripley Hitchcock insisted that Crane make these extensive changes a year later in spring 1895, after Crane had returned from his trip to the West and Mexico. The matter is further complicated by the question of what version of the novel did Crane and Hitchcock work with as they prepared the book for publication. Was it the original manuscript that Garland had read, which now contained corrections and crossed-out corrections; was it a carbon copy of the typescript made for the Bacheller syndicate's serialization of the novel in newspapers; or was it a new typescript made in spring 1895 following Hitchcock's supposed mandate for change? Despite the controversy that these questions have raised, there is no concrete evidence that Hitchcock ever saw the manuscript. The deleted chapter endings in the manuscript, which Parker and Binder have inferred that Hitchcock forced Crane to remove, do not appear in a version of *The Red Badge* that Hitchcock did actually see, the newspaper serialization. Soon after Crane sent him newspaper clippings of the serialization, Hitchcock accepted *The Red Badge* for publication by Appleton. As Fredson Bowers has concluded, "the deleted chapter endings were thus initiated solely by Crane and represent his last intention before he ordered the pre-Hitchcock final typescript and carbon.... Every piece of evidence indicates that the manuscript was not touched in any way after the typescript and its carbon were made from it except to abstract a few pages of a battle scene for separate magazine publication. A recent edition of *The Red Badge* trumpeting the reprinting of these repetitious chapter endings as the restoration of Crane's true intention from Hitchcock's requested deletion is just plain wrong. The evidence of the manuscript clearly shows that it was Crane who on his own initiative deleted them and wisely so" (Bowers 102). Today, most critics agree that the 1895 Appleton edition is the one readers should use, and this is the one that publishers have generally made available. An exception is Avon, which published in 1986 a version of *The Red Badge* based on the manuscript and advertised it as "The Only Complete Edition from the Original Manuscript" and the "*Red Badge* as Crane Actually Wrote It"; however, unless one accepts Hershel Parker's and Henry Binder's argument that Ripley Hitchcock forced Crane to cut the manuscript extensively, this is an unauthoritative version of the text.

Textual critics thus play an important role in the study of literature. In attempting to reconstruct as closely as possible what an author wanted an audience to read, they are at the forefront in helping readers appreciate a nation's literary heritage.

NOTE

1. Ironically, the Confederate General Thomas "Stonewall" Jackson was also wounded by his own men during the battle and died shortly thereafter.

7

Other War Stories

Crane's fiction about war falls into three chronological periods.[1] The first period deals with his fictional representations of battle before he had been in combat and includes *The Red Badge of Courage* (1895), *The Little Regiment and Other Episodes of the American Civil War* (1896), and "An Episode of War" (written 1896, first published 1899). These pieces are mostly impressionistic studies of fear and isolation or sentimental treatments of war. Between the first and second period is a transitional story, "Death and the Child," about the Greek-Turkish War in 1897. Like his earlier war stories, it focuses on an inexperienced soldier like Henry Fleming in *The Red Badge* or Fred Collins in "A Mystery of Heroism" who naively tries to make sense of war, but it is Crane's first story after having actually witnessed combat. By the time that Crane had been in the Spanish-American War in 1898, the second period, he had come to admire seasoned, professional veterans who did their task in combat dutifully and stoically; Crane paid tribute to them in *Wounds in the Rain* (1900). His final period occurred during the last year of his life, when he wrote a series of tales about an imaginary war between two fictitious countries, Spitzbergen and Rostina. Collected posthumously in *Last Words* (1902), these tales depict the anguish of war and the respect for individuals caught up in it. A common trait, however, runs throughout all of Crane's war fiction. Unlike other novelists like Émile Zola or Leo Tolstoy, Crane is not interested in the causes of war or the political and philosophical issues raised by it. Rather, he depicts it as a metaphor for the struggle of existence itself. As Chester L. Wolford has observed, "[g]iven how ill he was and how deep in debt, it is remarkable that these stories are so spare (he was paid by the word), so pessimistic (tubercular people tend to have visions of grand enterprise at the end), and that any of them is any good at all. And one, 'The Upturned Face,' is very good indeed" (*Short Fiction* 77).

FIRST PERIOD: STORIES ABOUT THE CIVIL WAR

To capitalize on the success of *The Red Badge of Courage,* S. S. McClure sent Crane to Virginia in late January 1896 to tour Civil War battlefields for a series of sketches about major battles for McClure's literary syndicate, but nothing came of the project. Instead, Crane wrote short stories about the war. He soon realized, however, that he could not sustain the narrative intensity of the novel. Fearing he had "used [himself] up in the accursed 'Red Badge,'" he wrote, "[p]eople may just as well discover now that the high dramatic key of *The Red Badge* cannot be sustained" (*Correspondence* 161, 191). Most of the stories were published as *The Little Regiment and Other Episodes of the American Civil War.*

THE LITTLE REGIMENT AND OTHER EPISODES OF THE AMERICAN CIVIL WAR

Crane published six stories in *The Little Regiment and Other Episodes of the American Civil War* (1896). Three of them are minor pieces lacking the imaginative quality often found in his fiction. "An Indiana Campaign," a humorous account of mistaken identity concerning the theft of chickens, was rejected by the *Atlantic Monthly* because "in substance it is somewhat too slight for our more or less serious pages" (*Correspondence* 226). "A Grey Sleeve," which concerns a nascent romance between a dashing Union officer and a Southern belle during combat, may have been written in response to the popularity of sentimental wartime love stories at the time. Although Crane once characterized their behavior as "charming in their childish faith in each other," they were "a pair of idiots," and "A Grey Sleeve" was "not in any sense a good story" (180, 171). In "Three Miraculous Soldiers," another Southern heroine helps three Confederate soldiers escape from the enemy. Despite its sentimental overtones, the story has drawn critical attention for the impressionistic technique in which the heroine's mental state restricts her sensory perception of reality. Almost the whole story is told from her narrow point of view in which she tries to understand what she sees. For example, when she perceives black dots on a road leading to her farm, she first interprets them as horsemen, but as she gets more aural and visual information, she realizes they are soldiers. Crane dramatizes the theme of limited perception when her vision is literally restricted as she peers through a knothole in the side of the barn. As James Nagel has observed, "the lengthy scenes based on what Mary can perceive through the knothole constitute one of the most remarkably limited narrative perspectives in American literature" (*Literary Impressionism* 48).

The three other stories in the collection are worth more detailed consideration. In the title story, "The Little Regiment," Dan and Billie Dempster are brothers who constantly bicker; however, the experience of combat makes them aware of how deeply they care for each other. When Billie is wounded and missing in action during a battle, Dan becomes depressed, but when they are reunited, there is an understated sense of relief. Throughout the story there is a blurring of fact and fiction. In a setting in which fog makes clothing "*seem* of a luminous quality" and have "*a kind of* blue" that "*might have been* merely a long, low shadow in the mist" (*Prose* 647, my emphasis), it is difficult to see clearly what is really there. The local town, "a faint etching upon the grey cloud-masses which were shifting with oily languor" (647), is like the ever-changing landscape that an impressionist painter tries to capture. A night that looks like "black velvet," a "fireless camp" that resembles "the faint drawings upon ancient tapestry," and the sheen of a rifle or button that becomes "threads of silver and gold sewn upon the fabric of the night" (655) reduce the setting to a woven work of art. In each of these examples, Crane emphasizes the irreducibility of nature and human experience to simple fact. Colors are constantly changing, nature is interchangeable with art, and attempts to record reality rely on slippery words like *seem* or *a kind of* or the subjunctive mood, as in *might have been*.

In "The Veteran," a sequel to *The Red Badge of Courage*, Henry Fleming recounts his battle experience to his grandson, whose "stout boyish idealism was injured" (667) upon learning that his grandfather had fled out of fear from the enemy during the Battle of Chancellorsville; however, Private Fleming must have become a respected veteran, for he was eventually promoted to orderly sergeant. When a Swedish hired hand gets drunk and accidentally sets a barn on fire, Fleming rushes in to save him and the animals but forgets about the colts. Returning to rescue them, he dies when the burning roof caves in.

John Berryman and Nicholas Delbanco offer Freudian readings to explain why Crane resurrected Henry Fleming from an earlier story. Berryman sees the story—as he does much of Crane's work—as an attempt to deal with Oedipal guilt toward his father, whose strict religious teachings Crane rebelled against. Crane uses two masks from previous stories—the indecisive Henry from *The Red Badge* and the terrified, death-obsessed Swede in "The Blue Hotel"—to represent himself in "The Veteran." When the older Henry rescues the Swede from the burning barn, Henry also represents Crane's father. In resolving the "aggression against his father, the wish to be the father, and the solution for panic" (Berryman, *Stephen Crane* 324), Crane allows the father/son mask of Henry to die heroically by rescuing the son mask of the Swede. Furthermore, as Berryman points out, Freud asserted that horse imagery is often associated with Oedipal guilt, hence the appropriateness that Henry should try to save horses. Delbanco broadens the psychological reading by associating the story with the "guilt of the survivor that . . . is characteristic of those American authors who missed the Civil War." Even though Crane was obviously born too late to have fought during the war, he had difficulty resolving this fact. In *The Red Badge,* Fleming is "at the edge of action only, a pampered child. The pale cast of thought has sicklied him." But because "conscience can make heroes of us all," Crane creates a situation for Fleming in "The Veteran" in which he can die heroically, an act that also brings closure to Crane's own anxiety at having not been in the war (Delbanco 50).

Unlike Berryman and Delbanco, Michael Fried offers a postmodernist interpretation to explain Crane's decision to bring Henry Fleming back. Because texts are indeterminate, a postmodernist would argue, any attempt to get at one meaning that unifies any text is bound to fail. For Fried, the inability of critics to agree upon the meaning of the ending of *The Red Badge*—has Fleming matured or is he still deluding himself?—is an excellent example of an indeterminate text. Nevertheless, a reader of a text constantly wants to make clear sense of it by reducing it to one meaning, a process that postmodernists call "totalizing." Fried infers that Crane, as a reader of his own text struggling to understand the ending of *The Red Badge,* wrote an unambiguous story, "The Veteran," in which Henry has "an ironic self-knowledge that far surpasses his most enlightened moments in the novel." In this sense, then, Crane is "the first (or among the first) of his totalizing readers, who traditionally have felt compelled to subsume under a univocal moral and/or psychological interpretation not only as many of the events of a given narrative as could be made to fit but also the overall shape of that narrative considered as a simultaneous unity" (160).

In addition to Freudian and postmodernist readings of "The Veteran," critics have explored the imagery, style, and structure. James B. Colvert connects the demonic imagery that describes the enemy in *The Red Badge* and the barn in the story to argue that Henry has finally confronted the demons that earlier had haunted him. Colvert also shows how the story reveals Crane's developing style. Whereas the novel resonates with "rhetorical flourishes [and] the studied elaboration of chiaroscuro imagery" of the author's early work, the short story typifies the "lean, open, disciplined prose" of his later years (Colvert, *Tales of War* xxviii–xxix). James Nagel gives a more extended analysis of the unity of the story. The first paragraph introduces serene images that later signify alarm. A horse that swishes its tail idly becomes a concern for horses in the barn; the visual image of the church belfry becomes aural as the bell is rung to alert the community to the fire; and the tranquil, yellow sunshine becomes the yellow flames of fire. Similarly, the imagery at the end associates the story with battle imagery in *The Red Badge*. The fire flames, like the regimental flag that Henry carries into battle, wave like a "banner"; Henry rushes into the smoke as he did at Chancellorsville; and he gets another red badge of courage when a horse breaks his hip. The effect of the imagery is to unify a loosely structured story and to reveal a clear pattern from Henry's cowardice in the novel to his heroism in the short story (*Literary Impressionism* 136–39).

The theme of heroism is further explored in "A Mystery of Heroism." During a fierce artillery battle between Union and Confederate forces, Fred Collins of Company A decides to take several canteens to get water for himself and his comrades from a nearby well on the battlefield. He soon realizes, however, the foolishness of his impulsive decision. When his comrades sense that Collins is having second thoughts about trying to get water under fire, they playfully jeer him on: "'Well, if yeh want a drink so bad, why don't yeh go git it?'" (*Prose* 625). Though an apparent need to save face prompts him to finally go for the water, he recognizes how dangerous the mission is: "he was suddenly smitten with terror. It came upon his heart like the grasp of claws" (629). Impatient with the slowness of filling canteens separately, he hastily fills a water bucket and runs back toward his company "in the manner of a farmer chased out of a dairy by a bull" (630). On the way he meets a wounded officer partly trapped under his horse who asks for a drink of water. At first he ignores him but then tries to give him water, only to have his shaking hands splash the water on the dying man's face. When he returns to his company, he gives the bucket to "two genial, sky-larking young lieutenants" (631). When one of them tries to take a drink, the other playfully jostles his elbow and knocks the bucket to the ground, spilling the water.

The story raises a question about the nature of bravery, a topic that fascinated Crane. He believed in what Ernest Hemingway, a great admirer of Crane, would later characterize as "grace under pressure," the ability to act stoically and resolutely during times of stress. Henry Fleming seems to have it in "The Veteran" as he runs into the barn, even though onlookers exclaim that his decision is "sure death" (670). In *The Red Badge,* however, the matter is not so clear cut. Judging from the reaction of colleagues, Henry acts heroically in battle, but to the narrator his actions are delirious. As a reading of the novel suggests, what one person defines as courage, another defines as irrational. In "A Mystery of Heroism," the matter is more complicated, for the definition of bravery as a heroic action consciously performed for altruistic reasons seems inappropriate in this story. More specifically, is Collins a hero for risking his life to get water for his comrades, or is he a fool carelessly motivated by pride? One might argue that his decision ultimately to comfort the dying officer suggests his empathy for fellow humans, but his action, whatever motivates it, is for naught. Perhaps the emptiness of the bucket symbolizes the emptiness of his action—and by extension, if actions have no meaning, does it imply the ultimate meaninglessness of abstractions such as courage and bravery? Hemingway would later echo the same sentiment in *A Farewell to Arms* when Frederic Henry, wearied from the ultimate uselessness of war, says, "I was always embarrassed by the words sacred, glorious, and sacrifice and the expression in vain. . . . Abstract words such as glory, honor, courage, or hallow were obscene" (184, 185). For many of Crane's and Hemingway's characters, the final question is, what is the proper mode of conduct in a chaotic universe?

"AN EPISODE OF WAR"

At the time that Crane was writing the stories that would be collected in *The Little Regiment,* he also composed one of his finest stories about war, "An Episode of War." Though written specifically for the *Youth's Companion* and submitted for publication in March 1896, it did not appear during Crane's lifetime probably because the editor feared that children might be offended by the harsh treatment of war. The magazine did, however, publish it in 1916 during World War I, thus implying a change in editorial policy regarding suitable material for the magazine. Before then, the British magazine *The Gentlewoman* had published the story in December 1899, and it was reprinted in *Last Words* (1902). At one point Crane titled the story "A Loss of an Arm: An Episode of War."

The story opens with a domestic scene on the battlefield during which the lieutenant, while using his sword to separate portions of coffee beans for the troops, is suddenly shot in the right arm. Because he is wearing his scabbard on the left side of his body, he needs a soldier to help him sheath the sword. Finding himself incapacitated, he is forced to leave the battlefield. As he heads for the field hospital, "he was enabled to see many things which as a participant in the fight were unknown to him" (*Prose* 672). This literally enlarged perspective is a metaphor for the shift in his attitude toward battle and life in general:

> A wound gives strange dignity to him who bears it. Well men shy from this new and terrible majesty. It is as if the wounded man's hand is upon the curtain which hangs before the revelations of all existence— the meaning of ants, potentates, wars, cities, sunshine, snow, a feather dropped from a bird's wing; and the power of it sheds radiance upon a bloody form, and makes the other men understand sometimes that they are little. (672)

When he reaches the hospital—appropriately located in a schoolhouse, a place where one goes to learn—he sees a wounded man calmly smoking a pipe, resigned to his condition. After the amputation of his arm, he returns home to his family grieving "at the sight of the flat sleeve." "Shamefaced" by their tears, the lieutenant says, "I don't suppose it matters so much as all that" (675).

The lieutenant's stoic resignation at the end of the story reveals an acceptance of his—or anyone else's—insignificance in the universe. As with the pipe smoker, a wound is a badge reminding them of their own mortality. Though it would be wrong to simply read Crane's fiction autobiographically, it is curious that in several stories like "An Episode of War" characters suddenly become aware of their own mortality. John Berryman has suggested that the central focus of these stories— "[h]ow to act, wounded" (*Stephen Crane* 256)—reflects Crane's awareness of his own mortality.[2] Sick as a child and adult, Crane had a weak constitution made only worse by his insistence that he personally experience what he wrote about, hence, for example, his living as a tramp to write "An Experiment in Misery." A number of his contemporaries compared him to Edgar Allan Poe insofar as being a literary genius fated to burn out quickly. After meeting Crane in 1895, Willa Cather recalled that "he had the precocity of those doomed to die in youth. I am convinced that when I met him he had a vague premonition of the shortness of his working day, and in the heart of the man there was that which said, 'That thou doest, do quickly'" (17).[3] Like the lieutenant, Crane recognized the fragility of life that could be irrevocably changed by such an insignificant detail as the distribution of coffee beans.[4]

TRANSITIONAL STORY: "DEATH AND THE CHILD"

Crane used his experience in the Greek-Turkish War in two works: *Active Service* and "Death and the Child." Whereas the novel uses war primarily as the setting for a domestic comedy of manners, the short story addresses a number of the larger issues about conflict and hero-ism treated in his more serious fiction about war. Besides being one of Crane's less-known masterpieces, it is also the first war story he wrote based on his actual experience of combat. The basis for the story is his war dispatch, "A Fragment of Velestino," a subjective newspaper account of the Battle of Velestino during the Greek-Turkish War. The fictional account of the battle, "Death and the Child," was published in London and New York in March 1898 and in the following month was included in the English and American editions of *The Open Boat.*

Peza—a young, Italian correspondent of Greek descent—has been assigned to report on the war. From the outset he clearly knows noth-ing about the reality of combat. "[I]n very nice tweed, with his new leggings, in his new white helmet, his new field-glass-case, his new revolver-holster," he is in stark contrast to "the soiled soldiers" "in their sticky brown trenches" (*Prose* 948). When he decides out of patriotism to fight with the Greeks, he adopts the "fiery dignity of a tragedian," melodramatically "declaim[s]" his lines, and accompanies them with "a sweeping gesture" (945). Like Henry Fleming in *The Red Badge of Courage,* Peza's view of war is based on his childlike imagination and an inflated sense of self-importance: "He remembered the pageants of carnage that had marched through the dreams of his childhood. Love he knew; that he had confronted alone, isolated, wondering, an indi-vidual, an atom taking the hand of a titanic principle" (947). The imme-diacy of war as well as the sight of dead and wounded, however, force Peza to confront his illusions about combat. He is upset when no one pays attention to "his protestations of high patriotism" and "exalted declarations" (956), and when duty requires that a lieutenant leave

Peza, the correspondent feels deserted and betrayed—conveniently forgetting that he chose to become a combatant—and plans "on some future occasion ... [to] take much trouble to arrange a stinging social revenge upon that grinning jackanapes" (953). In a scene reminiscent of several scenes in *The Red Badge* depicting Henry Fleming's plight, Peza comes face-to-face with a spectral soldier, whose "jaw had been half shot away" and whose breast "was drenched in blood." Confronted with the "mystic gaze" of impending death (957), Peza's only reaction, despite a plea from another soldier to help the dying man, is to run away.

Even though Peza tries to defend his actions or ignore the consequences of his behavior, the narrator constantly undercuts him. When Peza deserts the spectral soldier, the narrator quickly chastises him for being "surely craven in the movement of refusal" (957), and when he attempts to get a better viewpoint of the battle by standing on "a pillar" "surveying mankind, the world" (an image in which he ironically resembles a statue commemorating some military hero) (958), dust gets into Peza's eyes, literally and figuratively suggesting his own limited point of view.

Peza's limited perspective is contrasted with that of other characters. Experienced soldiers, though "certain to be heavily attacked before the day was old," remain calm: "The universities had not taught him to understand this attitude" (948). They have learned to accept the drudgery of war as essential to its outcome. As the dressing for wounds symbolically reveals—"the triangular kerchief, upon which one could still see, through the blood-stains, the little explanatory pictures illustrating the ways to bind various wounds. 'Fig. 1.' 'Fig. 2.' 'Fig. 7.'" (947)—war becomes a mechanical event in which one simply follows the numbers. Similarly, Peza's perspective is contrasted with that of a deserted child, whose confused parents, in the terrifying rush of innocent peasants to flee the battle, have forgotten him and left him in a hut on a hill. Like Peza, the child misreads the reality of war and interprets it only from the limited perspective of a child familiar with games and the actions of shepherds tending to a flock of animals. The narrator juxtaposes their two perspectives in the final section of the story, in which Peza finally gains a new perspective based on insight. The change is foreshadowed dramatically with "the readjustment of the sights" (962) of the rifles as the troops prepare to aim more accurately at the enemy.

Hungry and confused by the disappearance of his parents, the child cries; but when he sees Peza, exhausted and covered with dirt, dragging himself toward him, the child innocently asks twice, "Are you a man?"

From the child's perspective, this is a natural question, for his companion in the hut during the battle has been a cow, and in looking at the creature in front of him, "All the spick of [Peza's] former appearance had vanished in a general dishevelment, in which he resembled a creature that had been flung to and fro, up and down, by cliffs and prairies during an earthquake." From Peza's now-changed perspective, however, the question has a larger significance. Acknowledging the illusion of an inflated ego, he accepts his own insignificance in the grand scheme of the universe: "he confronted the primitive courage, the sovereign child, the brother of the mountains, the sky, and the sea, and he knew that the definition of his misery could be written on a wee grass-blade" (963).

As in *The Red Badge of Courage,* Crane contrasts the chaos of warfare with the sublime indifference of nature. As terrified peasants and animals flee from a battle scene—"as if fear was a river, and this horde had simply been caught in the torrent, man tumbling over beast, beast over man, as helpless in it as the logs that fall and shoulder grindingly through the gorges of a lumber country"—in the peaceful setting of nature, "one felt the existence of the universe scornfully defining the pain in ten thousand minds. The sky was an arch of stolid sapphire. Even to the mountains, raising their mighty shapes from the valley, this headlong rush of the fugitives was too minute" (943). Likewise, at the end of *The Red Badge,* the question of Henry Fleming's maturity is addressed: "He had been to touch the great death and found that, after all, it was but the great death. He was a man" (212). As pointed out earlier in the discussion of the novel, critics disagree as to whether to read the ending literally (that Henry has matured) or ironically (that he is still deluding himself). In "Death and the Child," however, Crane uses a question, "Are you a man?" rather than a declarative statement to suggest ironically that maturity has less to do with a conventional view of bravery and manhood than it does with the acceptance of one's own insignificance in the larger scheme of things. Like the lieutenant in "An Episode of War," Peza has learned from his experience. Because "Death and the Child" is Crane's first war story written from personal experience, perhaps he had begun to mature in his own view on the terrifyingly senseless nature of war.

SECOND PERIOD: *WOUNDS IN THE RAIN*

Of the more than 200 reporters, photographers, and artists who covered the Cuban phase of the Spanish-American War, Stephen Crane was among the two or three most famous—and arguably the best.

Hired in April 1898 by the *New York World* as their star correspondent, he was fired in July for reasons that are still not totally clear. Upon his dismissal, he was immediately hired by the rival *New York Journal* to report on the Puerto Rican campaign of the war. His dispatches, some of them of exceptional quality, cover the major events of the war, including the marine landing at Guantánamo Bay and the Battle of San Juan Hill. Following the war, Richard Harding Davis characterized "the best correspondent ... [as] probably the man who by his energy and resources sees more of war, both afloat and ashore, than do his rivals, and who is able to make the public see what he saw"; Crane "distinctly won the first place" (941).

Crane's experience in Cuba led to a collection of 11 war stories, *Wounds in the Rain*. As in his earlier war fiction, Crane continued to develop innovative narrative techniques and to explore the complex nature of courage and sacrifice, but unlike his earlier work, these stories are more firmly grounded in current social and political issues. In "The Price of the Harness," for example, which fictionalizes the American attack upon the fortifications of San Juan on July 1, 1898, Crane criticized the constant attention paid in the American press to colorful volunteer regiments such as Theodore Roosevelt's Rough Riders at the expense of the common, regular soldier. Instead of gloating over "the gallantry of Reginald Marmaduke Maurice Montmorenci Sturtevant, and for goodness sake how the poor old chappy endures that dreadful hard-tack and bacon," the press should report "the name of the regular soldier," named "Michael Nolan" by Crane, "the sweating, swearing, overloaded, hungry, thirsty, sleepless Nolan, tearing his breeches on the barbed wire entanglements, wallowing through the muddy fords, pursuing his way through the stiletto-pointed thickets, climbing the fire-crowned hill" (*Prose* 1013, 1014). Crane portrays regular, unsung soldiers who do their job quietly and responsibly with "marvelous impassivity" (1019). Rather than expecting that their actions will automatically gain them "encrusted medals from war" (1016), they do their duty with what Ernest Hemingway would later characterize as "grace under pressure." Despite Crane's admiration for common army privates during combat, the tone never becomes chauvinistic, and the story ends sardonically with a delirious soldier singing "The Star-Spangled Banner" to dying and fever-stricken soldiers. Similarly, "The Second Generation" criticizes nepotism and class privilege as the basis for a military commission. Senator Cadogan manipulates the political system to get his pampered son, Caspar, who is "resolved to go to the tropic wars and do something" (1108), a position as an army captain and commissary officer. To the narrator, however, appointing an inexperienced blue blood like Caspar as an officer has "all the logic of going to sea in a bathing-machine" (1109). When the troops land at Siboney, this "selfish young pig" (1113) spends much of his time looking for his missing saddle bags and eating other people's rations. In contrast to the unrealistic view of volunteers like Caspar who see war as a game or heroic adventure are the regular army signalmen in "Marines Signalling under Fire at Guantánamo," who calmly stand up in the line of fire to call in artillery shells from nearby ships.

Other stories debunk the attempt by newspapers to sensationalize commonplace events during the Cuban War. In "God Rest Ye, Merry Gentlemen," a correspondent is sent home for not producing yellow journalism (a term used to describe sensationalized news reporting). In "This Majestic Lie," Cuban and Spanish newspapers proclaim that the American fleet was defeated at Manila Bay and that "[t]he inhabitants of Philadelphia had fled to the forests ... Boston was besieged by the Apaches ... [and] Chicago millionaires were giving away their palaces for two or three loaves of bread" (1130–31). American journalism was not much better: "if the news arrived at Key West as a mouse, it was often enough cabled north as an elephant." In "The Lone Charge of William B. Perkins," Crane satirizes incompetent correspondents who have "no information of war and no particular rapidity of mind for acquiring it" and who "could not distinguish between a five-inch quick-firing gun and a pickle-plated ice-pick" (*Works* 6: 114). When a correspondent named Perkins thinks he sees a Spanish solider behind a bush, he grabs a rifle and foolishly runs toward him like "an almshouse idiot plunging through hot crackling thickets," only to discover that the supposed enemy is actually a "dried palm-branch" (116, 117). Perkins is further embarrassed when, caught in cross fire, he is forced to hide in a rusty, old, metal drum.

As with "The Lone Charge of William B. Perkins," "The Sergeant's Private Madhouse" portrays the absurdist humor that can erupt unexpectedly during combat. A sergeant discovers that a private assigned as a sentry at an outpost has apparently gone mad expecting the enemy to attack. When fighting does begin, the American troops almost run out of ammunition. Just as they are close to losing the battle, the private suddenly begins singing loudly a medley of songs. Amazed by his bizarre behavior, both sides stop shooting. Though the private is sent home to be treated for his mental condition, the narrator suggests that he was not as mad as the "March Hare" (174) but simply drunk.

Besides treating the war realistically and satirically, Crane experiments with innovative narrative techniques. Certainly one of his most stylistically and thematically complex stories is "The Clan of No-Name," which he called "a peach. I love it devotedly" (*Correspondence* 379). Its structure relies on frames. The story is prefaced by a seven-line poem in which the first and last lines are the same. Similarly in the nine-part story, the first and last parts concentrate on courtship scenes in Tampa, Florida, involving a fickle, young woman named Margharita. Parts one and nine frame parts two and eight, which focus on Spain's perspective on the Cuban War. At the center of the story is the combat action in parts three to seven. Just as the poem challenges readers to "Unwind my riddle" (*Prose* 1033) about the nature of heroism, the story requires them to make sense of complex details that link the poem and the nine parts of the story thematically and metaphorically. Margharita is involved in two relationships: one with Mr. Smith, a greedy American businessman; the other with Manolo Prat, a loyal lieutenant with the Cuban insurgents. While fighting the enemy, Prat gets trapped as he intentionally puts himself in harm's way to help troops even though he knows that he will probably die as a result of his action. Rather than thinking only of himself, he acts dutifully to help others and dies in combat because "[t]here was a standard and he must follow it" (1041). At the end of the story, Margharita accepts Mr. Smith's marriage proposal and burns her photograph of Manolo. Although Crane admires the common soldier's devotion to duty in other stories in *Wounds in the Rain,* in "The Clan of No-Name" he is ambivalent about the ultimate value of Manolo's actions in which, within 30 minutes during his first battle, Manolo accomplishes nothing, kills no one, gets shot and hacked to death, and has his possessions stolen, only later to be forgotten by Margharita. Would a more mindful soldier such as the seasoned veteran who describes Manolo's actions as "desperate and careless" (1041) have avoided a position of near-certain death? Is the destruction of the photo a sign of Margharita's callousness? And is the narrator mocking Manolo's foolishness? To attempt to answer these questions, readers must confront the complex plot, shifting points of view and time schemes, and the indeterminacy of meaning that make "The Clan of No-Name" a precursor to postmodernism.

Although several stories in *Wounds in the Rain* are memorable depictions of war, the masterpiece is "War Memories," by far the longest story in the collection. Unlike other autobiographical accounts of the war that focus on factual summaries of military details and major events, in "War Memories" Crane, adopting the persona of a correspondent named Vernall, presents impressionistic accounts of his own experience of combat. As experimental stylistically as *The Red Badge of Courage,* "War Memories" blurs the line between fact and fiction and dramatizes an author trying to make sense of himself and struggling with ontological and linguistic questions about the nature of reality.

At the outset Vernall acknowledges the inability to capture objective truth, "the real thing," because "'war is neither magnificent nor squalid; it is simply life, and an expression of life can always evade us. We can never tell life, one to another, although sometimes we think we can.'" Rather, he constantly reminds the reader about the ironies of war. When Vernall and other correspondents are on a dispatch boat headed for Cuba, the immediate danger is not from "heavy seas" or enemy fire but from "a huge bunch of bananas, which ... hung like a chandelier in the centre of the tiny cabin." When the bananas almost knock one of the correspondents overboard and send another one crashing into a corner, Vernall sees the whimsical humor in the attempt to get at "the real thing" about war: "You see? War! A bunch of bananas rampant because the ship rolled" (*Works* 6: 222).

At times Vernall is a comical hero simply trying to survive. He worries all day about his lost toothbrush and berates himself for being "a blockhead" (239) when he realizes that he should have washed his own dishes after eating with troops. After he experiences combat, he inflates his own importance as a war correspondent and expects special treatment at a hotel in Port Antonio, Jamaica: "'I shall have a great bath and fine raiment, and I shall dine grandly and there will be lager beer on ice. And there will be attendants to run when I touch a bell, and I shall catch every interested romantist in the town, and spin him the story of the fight at Cusco'"(234–35). His grandiose expectations, however, are met with incredulity by a hotel manager and a clerk and with mild amusement by a guest who simply asks, "'Who is that chap in the very dirty jack boots?'" (235). In contrast to his self-deflating humor and whimsical treatment of war, however, is his graphic depiction of the agonizing death of an officer "dying hard," whose breathing "as all noble machinery breathes when it is making its gallant strife against breaking," was like "the noise of a heroic pump which strives to subdue a mud which comes upon it in tons. The darkness was impenetrable. The man was lying in some depression within seven feet of me. Every wave, vibration, of his anguish beat upon my senses" (226–27).

Like "The Clan of No-Name," "War Memories" foreshadows postmodern conceptions of language and narrative technique. Throughout, the narrator is self-consciously aware of his ultimate inability to make sense of his limited perception of "the real thing." Occasionally, he realizes that "[he has] forgotten to tell you" an important detail; at other times, in trying to recall simple details about his experience in Cuba, he has only a "vague sense" or "vague impression" of his war memories (247, 248, 249)—certainly a contrast to Theodore Roosevelt's autobiographical *The Rough Riders,* in which the author appeared to have total recall of even the smallest detail. As a result, the chronology in "War Memories" is complex. Vernall's inability to control his narrative is further complicated by his implied conversation with an unnamed, voiceless interlocutor who wants the narrator to tell heroic stories about the Rough Riders and the military details about the famous battles at Las Guásimas and the San Juan hills—the kind of narrative that Roosevelt and others wrote. This narrative battle between an uncertain narrator and an audience demanding romantic accounts of glorious deeds highlights the ontological and linguistic difficulties in trying to capture "the real thing" in the act of storytelling itself.

Vernall learns that language cannot ultimately articulate what is real about war—or anything. As he proclaims in the first paragraph, "'It seems impossible!'" (222). Nearly 20,000 words later, as Vernall looks back upon his story, all he can say with certainty is that "[t]he episode was closed. And you can depend upon it that I have told you nothing at all, nothing at all, nothing at all" (263)—and yet paradoxically he gives us a disturbing glimpse at an "overwhelming, crushing, monstrous" (254) reality so different from that in other accounts of the Spanish-American War. One of America's greatest accounts of war, "War Memories" foreshadows Hemingway's artistic dictum in *Death in the Afternoon* to get "the real thing" (2) in writing as well as postmodern narratives of the Vietnam War, most notably Michael Herr's *Dispatches* (Robertson 174).

Though Crane wrote the stories in *Wounds in the Rain* at least partly to pay for his mounting personal debts, he was concerned about their literary integrity. When a magazine editor changed the title of "The Price of the Harness," for example, Crane protested because of the importance of the title for understanding "the price the men paid for wearing the military harness" (*Correspondence* 387). Based on his personal notes, it is clear that he envisioned the 11 stories published in *Wounds in the Rain* in 1900 as a unified group linked thematically by what he called "the singular and sinister brutality of the title" (595, n. 1).

As he wrote to his literary agent, "I spent two months trying to find an effective title to the book of War Stories.... This seemed to me very effective.... [T]he books on the Cuban War have for more than a year terrified the Stokes firm and they have not the slightest idea that they are now in possession of the only fairly decent book on the Cuban War which has yet been written" (595). Crane clearly saw his book as an alternative to the literary jingoism that had flooded the market since the end of the war.

Crane's contemporaries praised stories in *Wounds in the Rain.* Joseph Conrad called "The Price of the Harness" "magnificent" and "the very best thing [Crane] has done since the Red Badge" (396), and Richard Harding Davis identified "Marines Signalling under Fire at Guantánamo" as the best account of an event during the war. Modern critics have also recognized the excellence of several of the stories. Patrick K. Dooley considered "The Clan of No-Name" a "stunning achievement" (34), and John Berryman admired the "undiminished power of conception and execution" in "Virtue in War" and its "laconic perfection of mannerless phrasing which is one ideal of our prose since Crane" (*Stephen Crane* 252, 253).

THIRD PERIOD: "THE SPITZBERGEN TALES"

In 1899 Crane wrote four stories called "The Spitzbergen Tales" about a war between two fictitious countries, Spitzbergen and Rostina. The stories focus on an infantry regiment called the Kicking Twelfth. There is a narrative progression in them, and in three of the stories the main character is Lieutenant Timothy Lean. In "The Kicking Twelfth," Lieutenant Lean defeats the enemy from Rostina despite suffering heavy losses. In "The Shrapnel of Their Friends," during a second engagement with the enemy, the regiment accidentally comes under artillery fire from one of its own batteries. Despite the reality of war, the stories contain a touch of humor: Colonel Sponge is named after one of Crane's dogs, and Major General Richie is named after Edith Richie (Jones), a houseguest of the Cranes to whom Stephen dictated the first story.

In "And If He Wills, We Must Die," however, the mood is more bleak. During intense and chaotic fighting, Rostina troops annihilate a squad of Spitzbergen soldiers who were defending a house at the front of enemy lines. Their death is depicted with the kind of graphic detail reminiscent of the descriptions of dying and dead soldiers in *The Red Badge of Courage:* "a man was shot in the throat. He gurgled and then lay down on the floor. The blood slowly waved down the brown skin of his neck while he looked meekly at his comrades" (*Prose* 1279-80). When Sergeant Morton reloads his rifle, he accidentally slips "in the blood of the man who had been shot in the throat," and his boot makes "a greasy red streak on the floor" (1281). The last man to die, Morton looks at his wounded men and poignantly gasps the battle cry of the regiment: "Kim up, the Kickers." When the enemy enters the house and sees "the scene of blood and death," a soldier pays tribute to the courage of the fallen: "'God! I should have estimated them as at least one hundred strong'" (1282). The reader, however, is aware of the final tragic irony: the battle was unnecessary, for a courier had been sent with orders for the squad to retreat, but he had been killed before he could reach the house.

"THE UPTURNED FACE"

The best of the Spitzbergen tales and Crane's final comment on the tragedy of war is "The Upturned Face." During combat, Lieutenant Timothy Lean, an adjutant, and two privates are burying one of their comrades. Frightened by the corpse as much as by enemy fire, they are forced to look at and touch the body. While the lieutenant and adjutant lower the body into the grave, they stumble into it, and when they try to recite the service of the dead, they cannot remember all of the words, although ironically the ones they do remember are for burial at sea. When one of the privates is wounded while shoveling dirt into the grave, Lean orders the privates to retreat to the rear and begins to cover up the corpse. As he shovels "frantically" and with "a gesture of abhorrence," the dirt landing on the corpse makes "a sound—plop" until there is "nothing to be seen but the chalk-blue face" (*Prose* 1286). When the adjutant beseeches him to finish the burial, "Lean swung back the shovel; it went forward in a pendulum curve. When the earth landed it made a sound—plop" (1287).

This is a richly evocative story because of its autobiographical connections and stylistic techniques. The story is partly based on the death of marine surgeon John Blair Gibbs, whom Crane had befriended during the Spanish-American War. One night while idly standing beside his tent, Gibbs became one of the first American casualties of the war when he was shot by sniper fire. Crane was close enough to him to witness his slow but agonizing death. The next day he and several others buried Gibbs and conducted a funeral service that, as in "The Upturned Face," was under enemy gunfire. The horrifying experience haunted

Crane, and he reported it in one of his war dispatches from Cuba and later in "War Memories."

In terms of technique, "The Upturned Face" is practically unlike any other war story that Crane wrote. A number of the basic elements of fiction—in particular, plot, setting, visual imagery, and point of view—have been kept to a minimum. The narrator is detached, and there is almost no action, no description of where the characters are, or no clear sense of what time of day it is. Typically, Crane's stories rely on visual images to help convey mood, theme, and character; however, here there are few: the dead man's face, his clothing, and his few possessions. Instead, Crane focuses on aural and tactile imagery: the attempt to avoid touching the corpse and the sound of dirt dropping onto it. The story is the best example of Crane's late prose style, which, as characterized by James B. Colvert, is "lean, open, and sardonically understated." The style allows Crane to refine "his essentially mythic sense of war so severely that it seems all but absent except in the broad context of his characteristic feeling for the ambiguous crossing of horror and humor in a dreamlike suspension of the movement of time" ("Style as Invention" 131).

The image of an upturned face is a recurring motif throughout Crane's fiction. In "When Man Falls, a Crowd Gathers," an account of a man having an epileptic seizure on the streets of New York City, a fascinated and shocked crowd stares at his contorted face: "They seemed scarcely to breathe. They were contemplating a depth into which a human being had sunk and the marvel of this mystery of life and death held them chained" (*Prose* 601). In *The Red Badge,* Henry Fleming stares at the "ashen face" of the "invulnerable dead man ... the impulse of the living to try to read in dead eyes the answer to the Question" (102). Henry Johnson's disfigurement in "The Monster" is the result of chemicals that pour onto his "upturned face" (406). And Peza in "Death and the Child" feels "himself blanch" as he gazes intently at "[t]wo liquid-like eyes [that] were staring into his face.... [H]e was being drawn and drawn by these dead men, slowly, firmly down as to some mystic chamber under the earth" (961). Like all of these characters, Lieutenant Lean searches for the ultimate meaning of reality in the glazed stare of a speechless body.

As with the image of "the chalk-blue face" that the lieutenant looks at, Crane's use of blue, as with Herman Melville's use of white to depict the whale in *Moby-Dick,* often represents the unknowable as well as one's insignificance in a naturalistic universe. In Crane's poem "If I should cast off this tattered coat," the narrator considers that there is nothing beyond the immediate reality of one's existence except "a vast blue, / Echoless, ignorant,— / What then?" (1323). Regarding "himself merely as a part of a vast blue demonstration," Henry Fleming at one point notices that the dying, tattered soldier's "face had turned to a shade of blue" and at another is surprised that, during hectic combat, nature, with its "blue, pure sky and the sun gleamings on the trees and fields ... had gone tranquilly on with her golden process in the midst of so much devilment" (86, 138, 116). In "The Open Boat," which presents characters recognizing their own insignificance in the universe, "the color of the sky" is "pure blue" (885, 905). And in "The Blue Hotel," wherein the color of the hotel and "the snow turning blue in the shadow of dusk" suggest the mystery of existence, humans are merely "lice ... caused to cling to a whirling, fire-smote, ice-locked, disease-stricken, space-lost bulb" (804, 822).

"The Upturned Face" can be read not only as one of Crane's last stories but also as a summation of his philosophy of life. Lieutenant Lean and the adjutant try with great difficulty to maintain some sense of propriety and dignity as they struggle to give meaning to a ceremonial burial of a comrade. They discover, however, that any attempt to assign significance to a ceremony—indeed, any ceremony—is meaningless in a chaotic universe. Nevertheless, humans need to adhere to a code of conduct, what George W. Johnson calls Crane's "metaphor of decorum" (250). Though humans are trapped between "an unknowable world and incongruous ceremonies," says Johnson, they still believe in these ceremonies because it allows them to "accept incongruities which would otherwise overwhelm [their] imagination" (251, 253). A code of conduct maintains at least a semblance of order and civility. In his war fiction, Crane has moved from Henry Fleming's self-absorbed, romanticized view of combat in *The Red Badge of Courage,* through the larger social and historical concerns of war in *Wounds in the Rain,* to the final suspension of humanity between an unknowable universe and incongruous rituals. In this sense, Crane is a precursor of what will become a dominant theme in twentieth-century fiction: the sense of isolation and alienation in an inhospitable world.

NOTES

1.   Crane also wrote a number of war sketches and dispatches about the Greek-Turkish War and the Spanish-American War. *Great Battles of the World* (1901) contains eight articles on major battles; however, Kate Lyon, Harold

Frederic's mistress and a friend of the Cranes, did the research and wrote most of the eight articles.

2.   Berryman mistakenly thought that the story was written in 1899; however, it was written in 1896. His confusion may have resulted from the fact that the story was published in December 1899 at a time when Crane was becoming increasingly ill. Nevertheless, his theory is still intriguing, given Crane's frail constitution.

3.   Nicholas Delbanco (49) also cites Cather to suggest Crane's concern with mortality.

4.   The American edition of this volume is titled *The Open Boat and Other Tales of Adventure*. The English edition, published simultaneously, is titled *The Open Boat and Other Stories* and contains an added section of stories.

8

Western Stories

After the abridged version of *The Red Badge of Courage* appeared in December 1894, Irving Bacheller hired Crane as a special correspondent to travel to the West and Mexico and to report on his experiences. Bacheller had been impressed with Crane's powers of observation in the novel and the positive response of readers to it. Crane left for four months starting in late January 1895. Though little is known about the facts of the trip, Willa Cather provided a dramatized account of her meeting him in February. Well before she would become famous as a novelist, Cather was at the time a student at the University of Nebraska and was working part-time for the *Nebraska State Journal.* She recalled,

> He gave me to understand that he led a double literary life; writing in the first place the matter that pleased himself, and doing it very slowly; in the second place, any sort of stuff that would sell.... The thing that most interested me was what he said about his slow method of composition. He declared that there was little money in story-writing at best, and practically none in it for him, because of the time it took him to work up his detail. Other men, he said, could sit down and write up an experience while the physical effect of it, so to speak, was still upon them, and yesterday's impressions made to-day's "copy." But when he came in from the streets to write up what he had seen there, his faculties were benumbed, and he sat twirling his

pencil and hunting for words like a schoolboy.... He declared that his imagination was hide-bound; it was there, but it pulled hard. After he got a notion for a story, months passed before he could get any sort of personal contact with it, or feel any potency to handle it. "The detail of a thing has to filter through my blood, and then it comes out like a native product, but it takes forever," he remarked. (Cather 15–16)

Cather's recollection about Crane's "slow method of composition" proved accurate, for it took more than three years after the Western trip for him to write two of his most famous stories, "The Bride Comes to Yellow Sky" and "The Blue Hotel."

"THE BRIDE COMES TO YELLOW SKY"

Published in early 1898, "The Bride Comes to Yellow Sky" is one of Crane's most frequently studied short stories. Marshal Jack Potter and his unnamed bride are returning by train to Yellow Sky after having just been married in San Antonio. Potter has told no one about the marriage and is hoping to get home privately to avoid any fanfare about it. Scratchy Wilson, who is "about the last one of the old gang that used to hang out along the river here" (*Prose* 794), has come to town drunk and is scaring everyone, including a local dog, with his wild shooting. In the past, Marshal Potter had been able to protect the town from Wilson's games of comic violence. People had come to accept their periodic confrontations as essentially harmless. But because Potter has not returned yet, "for the next two hours," as the barkeeper laments, "this town won't be a health resort" (792). The tension increases until Wilson confronts the newlywed couple before they get a chance to sneak home. What appears to be the setting for a shootout is immediately defused when Potter tells Scratchy that he does not have a gun. In an attempt to goad Potter into a fight, Scratchy sneers, "'If you ain't got a gun, why ain't you got a gun?' ... 'Been to Sunday-school?'" (797). But when Scratchy learns that his relationship with Potter has been forever changed because of the marriage, he cannot accept what it implies—the end of his game playing with Potter: "He was not a student of chivalry; it was merely that in the presence of this foreign condition he was a simple child of the earlier plains" (798).

Crane's story parodies the classic confrontation between lawman and outlaw that was so prevalent in popular Western fiction in the late nineteenth century. Rather than being an adventurous hero, Potter is an awkward, middle-aged marshal who suddenly decides he wants to get married. The decision, however, is far from easy for him. Fearing that he has somehow shunned his duty as a lawman by secretly getting married, he has convinced himself that "[h]e had committed an extraordinary crime" that "could only be exceeded by the burning of the new hotel" (789). His social awkwardness is obvious as he sits stiffly on the train shyly looking at other passengers and trying to make conversation with his bride, who, neither "pretty" nor "very young," was similarly embarrassed by her uncomfortable clothing and "by the careless scrutiny of some passengers" (787) who were amused by the newlyweds' social discomfort.

Their awkwardness notwithstanding, the marshal and his wife are part of a new wave of civilization that has been rapidly advancing across the American frontier. As the story opens, the narrator depicts an optical illusion to suggest the Easternization of the West: "The great Pullman was whirling onward with such dignity of motion that a glance from the window seemed simply to prove that the plains of Texas were pouring eastward. Vast flats of green grass, dull-hued spaces of mesquite and cactus, little groups of frame houses, woods of light and tender trees, all were sweeping into the east, sweeping over the horizon, a precipice" (787). Sitting on the train, one gets the feeling that the emblems of the once-rugged frontier were being swept away and that the environment geographically and culturally was at a turning point and the beginning of something new. As the train brings the newly married couple home, so too does it bring what marriage represents—family, domesticity, refinement—everything that the once-rugged West lacked. As a symbol of technological and cultural progress, the train appears like a palace or museum with "dazzling fittings ... sea-green figured velvet, the shining brass, silver, and glass, the wood that gleamed as darkly brilliant as the surface of a pool of oil ... a bronze figure ... [and] frescoes in olive and silver" (788). Given the end of one era in American history and the dawn of another, it is appropriate that the name of the town be associated with renewal, for "the hour of Yellow Sky, the hour of daylight, was approaching" (789).

Crane's depiction of a vanishing frontier in America reflected an enormously influential thesis developed by historian Frederick Jackson Turner in a speech, "The Significance of the Frontier in American History," given at the Columbian Exposition in Chicago in 1893. Turner examined how the West had shaped the character of the American people and believed, as did countless others, that by 1890, with the westward movement of culture, there was essentially no longer an unexplored, pristine frontier in America. After the speech was printed in an expanded form in 1894, hundreds of copies were sent to historians and intellectuals throughout the country. The *Atlantic Monthly* and other major journals featured articles on Turner's thesis, which today is still considered one of the seminal statements about American culture.

Despite this depiction of the rapid advancement of civilization across the continent, Scratchy Wilson still considers Yellow Sky a "deserted village" where a gun is man's best friend and where disputes are settled not in court but on the street. But even his attempt to hold on to an earlier way of life is undermined by his clothing—a "maroon-colored flannel shirt, which had been purchased for purposes of decoration and made, principally, by some Jewish women on the east side of New York" and his red, gilded boots, "the kind beloved in winter by little sledding boys on the hillsides of New England" (794)—which symbolizes the advancement of civilization onto the frontier. Simply put, it is hard to be taken seriously as an outlaw when you are wearing a decorative costume. It is no surprise, then, that Scratchy is dejected when he meets the newlyweds and discovers that Potter has at his side not a gun but a bride. Unable to accept the passing of the frontier, Scratchy can only say dejectedly, "'I s'pose it's all off now'" (798), referring to the ritualized games that he and the marshal had played. As one critic has noted, "When Scratchy makes funnel-shaped tracks in the heavy sand, time, in the shape of the hour glass, has caught up with him. The old West and the old code are gone forever" (Barnes, item 39). Ironically, as Frank Bergon demonstrates, Crane's burlesque of the classic showdown between lawman and outlaw foreshadows *The Virginian,* Owen Wister's 1902 best-selling novel that solidified the modern-day, Hollywood formula for a Western story.

Although much critical attention has been focused on the theme of East versus West in the story, the narrative structure has also gained attention. Overton P. James divides the story into four sections, each of which deals with the conflict between an old and new era. In the first section, which occurs on the train, the marshal and his bride try to adapt to the new era; in the second section, the action in the Weary Gentleman Saloon, Scratchy tries to hold on to the old way; in the third section, Scratchy's rampage through Yellow Sky, Wilson searches for an ally; and in the fourth section, the showdown, the old and new eras confront each other. While also recognizing a four-part structure, Robert G. Cook finds in it a visual pattern. The narrative structure "consists of two converging lines—the one beginning in the train in section one, the other beginning in the Weary Gentleman Saloon in section two" (369) with the two converging in section four. The imagery reinforces this converging pattern: the angle formed by the approaching train in one direction and by the mist rising off the Rio Grande in the other direction with Yellow Sky at the apex, Potter and Scratchy's meeting at right angles instead of head on in section four, and Scratchy's funnel-shaped tracks at the end visually depict lines of action moving toward a climax.

James Nagel expands upon the idea of a four-part structure by demonstrating that the episodic nature of the action reflects Crane's interest in Impressionism as an art form and as a way of understanding reality. In a fine summary of Impressionism, Nagel points out that

> [o]f all the aesthetic elements of Impressionistic fiction, structural organization serves as the most graphic indication of its unique characteristics. As in painting and music, the basic unit is a single moment of experience, what the French painters termed a *vistazo,* a "flash of perception," and what Ravel and Debussy transformed into abbreviated musical compositions. In fiction, this idea results in fragmentary episodes, brief scenes that require unique organization to give the total work a satisfying artistic order. If episodic progression is the controlling idea, the juxtaposition of scenes for emphasis and the arrangement of episodes into patterns provide strategies for variations of design. In short, the two informing principles are the demand for episodic units and the artistic arrangement of these fragmentary experiences into an aesthetically satisfying conception. (*Literary Impressionism* 124)

The fragmentary nature of many of Crane's stories reflects the fragmentary nature of experience in real life: "Life consists of episodes; psychologically realistic fiction must portray events as abbreviated units of apprehension rather than, as in Naturalism and Romanticism, a continuum of action that reveals a unified meaning about the universe." In "The Bride Comes to Yellow Sky," Crane links the fragments together to "provide important juxtapositions of events and ideas" (125). Thus, the first two sections, despite being disconnected in terms of plot, are connected in terms of the theme of "cultural displacements": Mr. and Mrs. Potter on the train and the drummer in the saloon are naive about their environment. In the third section there is "temporal displacement": Scratchy as gunfighter is in the right place but at the wrong time, for "time has passed him by." The final section dramatizes these displacements by shifting the time scheme to the present during the showdown between the past (Scratchy) and the future (the Potters). Despite fragmentation, "[s]een from its conclusion, the story is a model of unity: it combines two antithetical lines of action, focused on a common idea in four episodes, to form a confrontation of great, if comic, intensity. The result was one of the finest works Crane ever wrote and one of the most memorable pieces of fiction in American literature" (126).

"THE BLUE HOTEL"

Whereas "The Bride Comes to Yellow Sky" treats the passing of the West comically, "The Blue Hotel," published in late 1898, dramatizes the tragic consequences of attempting to hold on to it. During a fierce snowstorm, Patrick Scully, proprietor of the Palace Hotel in Fort Romper, meets a train passing through town, hoping to find customers for his establishment. He convinces three travelers to spend the night: Billy, a cowboy on his way to a ranch; Mr. Blanc, an Easterner; and an unnamed, "shaky and quick-eyed" (*Prose* 799) Swede. It quickly becomes clear that the Swede confuses the reality of the West with its romanticized portrayal in cheap fiction. As the Easterner observes, "'it seems to me this man has been reading dime-novels, and he thinks he's right out in the middle of it—the shootin' and stabbin' and all'" (809). During a card game at the hotel, the Swede unexpectedly announces that someone is going to kill him and plans to leave. Fearful of losing a customer, Scully tries to calm him down by talking to him alone and depicting Fort Romper as a civilized community soon to have electric streetcars, a new railroad line, "'[n]ot to mention the four churches and the smashin' big brick schoolhouse. Then there's the big factory, too. Why, in two years Romper'll be a met-tro-*pol*-is'" (807). Still convinced that he is in a dangerous place, the Swede tries to pay his hotel bill, but Scully refuses to take the money, instead showing him photos of two of his children and encouraging him to drink whisky. The alcohol, however, turns the Swede into a boisterous combatant. At supper, he "fizzed like a fire-wheel," "domineered the whole feast," and "gazed, brutally disdainful, into every face" (811), and when the card game resumes, the drunken Swede accuses Scully's son, Johnnie, of cheating. Their argument leads to a fistfight in which the Swede brutally beats up Johnnie. Forced to leave the hotel, the Swede wanders into a saloon and encounters local businessmen and a professional gambler. When the gambler refuses to drink with him, the Swede grabs him by the throat and drags him out of his chair. During a scuffle, the gambler kills the Swede by stabbing him.

Given the Swede's boisterous behavior, it seems appropriate that his corpse, "alone in the saloon, had its eyes fixed upon a dreadful legend that dwelt a-top of the cash-machine. 'This registers the amount of your purchase'" (826). Seemingly, the legend is telling readers that the Swede got what he paid for. Crane, however, does not end the story at this point. In a concluding section, readers learn important new information. When the cowboy asserts that the Swede was responsible for his own fate, the Easterner announces that the Swede was indeed correct in accusing Johnnie of cheating and not totally to blame for his own death:

> Johnnie was cheating. I saw him. I know it. I saw him. And I refused to stand up and be a man. I let the Swede fight it out alone. And you—you were simply puffing around the place and wanting to fight. And then old Scully himself! We are all in it! This poor gambler isn't even a noun. He is kind of an adverb. Every sin is the result of a collaboration. We, five of us, have collaborated in the murder of this Swede. Usually there are from a dozen to forty women really involved in every murder, but in this case it seems to be only five men—you, I, Johnnie, old Scully, and that fool of an unfortunate gambler came merely as a culmination, the apex of a human movement, and gets all the punishment. (827-28)

Then, the cowboy, "injured and rebellious, cried out blindly into this fog of mysterious theory. 'Well, I didn't do anythin', did I?'" (828).

"The Blue Hotel" is an especially rich story for analysis. Critics often focus on the naturalistic universe in which the action occurs. Lars Åhnebrink, for example, focuses on elements of fatalism and determinism (193), and Charles Child Walcutt sees the story as "a satire on causation" since the Swede is fated to die because of "his craven and ignorant heart" (75). The setting of the story certainly suggests an amoral world in which life has little, if any, ultimate significance. While the travelers take refuge in the Palace Hotel, the snowstorm outside rages on. Any attempt to find comfort and understanding among one's fellow humans, however, is futile:

> We picture the world as thick with conquering and elate humanity, but here, with the bugles of the tempest pealing, it was hard to imagine a peopled earth. One viewed the existence of man then as a marvel, and conceded a glamour of wonder to these lice which were caused to cling to a whirling, fire-smote, ice-locked, disease-stricken, space-lost bulb. The conceit of man was explained by this storm to be the very engine of life. One was a coxcomb not to die in it. (*Prose* 822)

The violent storm becomes a metaphor for the violent nature of humans, who, despite a veneer of respectability, are at heart as ruthless as animals. The fight between Johnnie and the Swede has "elements of leonine cruelty in it," and Scully yells at the Swede in "panther-fashion." In such a stormy setting, communication is impossible. When Scully yells at the Swede, "The wind tore the words from Scully's lips and scattered them far a-lee," and when the Swede tries to reply by saying, "'You are all a gang of—' ... the storm also seized the remainder of this sentence" (816).

Although the depiction of the universe and humanity in "The Blue Hotel" is bleak, Crane does not simply conclude that humans are amoral creatures controlled by deterministic forces over which they have no control; instead, there is an emphasis on what happens when people misread each other, when communication breaks down, and when individuals ignore the natural and ethical consequences of their actions. Though the Swede misreads the West because of his fondness for dime-novels, he sees through Johnnie's deception in the card game, and his attempt to leave the Palace Hotel soon after arriving reveals that he correctly senses the potential for violence there. The other characters are no better at reading reality than he is. When they have trouble understanding him, the cowboy dismisses the Swede with a racist stereotype: "'It's my opinion ... he's some kind of a Dutchman.' It was a venerable custom of the country to entitle as Swedes all light-haired men who spoke with a heavy tongue" (809). Johnnie dismisses him simply by saying, "I don't know nothin' about you ... and I don't give a damn where you've been" (803).

Although the Swede believes that he is fated to die in the Palace Hotel, it oversimplifies the matter, as the Easterner asserts, to conclude that only the gambler is responsible for his death. Legally, this is so because he killed the Swede, but morally (as depicted in grammatical terms), the gambler is not "a noun" but "an adverb": he is not the sole doer of the action but rather someone who modified an action already begun by others—the "five of us"—all of whom contribute in various ways to the tragic outcome of the story. Though Scully appears to be a congenial host taking care of his customers' needs, his motives are purely financial. To entice customers to his hotel, he is "a master of strategy" who "work[s] his seduction" on prospective customers (799), "practically [makes] them prisoners" (800), and paints his hotel a garish blue so that it is the first building seen after leaving the train station. Like his father, Johnnie also cares only about his own interests. His immediate reaction to charges of irresponsibility is denial. When his father accuses him of troubling the Swede, Johnnie decries defensively, "'Well, what have I done?'" (806), a question that foreshadows the last line of the story. Before the travelers arrive at the Palace Hotel, there is already tension in the air as a result of a card game between Johnnie and a farmer. Though the narrator does not tell us the cause of their disagreement, the farmer's "air of great impatience and irritation" (800) raises the possibility that he too suspects Johnnie of cheating, lending credence in hindsight to the Swede's charge. Similarly, though the cowboy denies any responsibility for his actions, he goads Johnnie on a half dozen times during the fight with the Swede to "[k]ill him" (817). Although the Easterner feebly tries to stop the fight, he too joins the cowboy and Scully in "a cheer that was like a chorus of triumphant soldiery" when Johnnie hits the Swede (818). Given the course of action in the story, who is responsible for the Swede's death? Whereas the law says that the gambler must serve three years in prison for his crime, "We, five of us, have collaborated in the murder of this Swede."

Critics have long debated the significance of the final section of the story. Should it be read as an affirmation of the need to assume responsibility for one's actions, is it an ironic statement about the ultimate meaninglessness of any human action in an amoral universe, or is it simply a tacked-on ending that unnecessarily complicates what seems obvious—that the Swede is responsible for his own death? Edwin H. Cady offers a useful commentary on the question:

> The final section, IX, has been a scandal and a stumbling block to no few commentators partly because it challenges a simply naturalistic reading of the story, partly because it explicitly introduces a moral idea and militates against the notion that Crane is always a nonideological symbolist in his art. Actually what the addition of the final page and a half does to the story is greatly to enrich it by deliberately reversing its moral perspectives and restoring them to the same challenging ambiguity between naturalistic and at least humanistic perspectives of "The Open Boat." (156)

For Cady, Crane is reflecting Tolstoy's view of Christianity as popularized in America in the novels of one of Crane's mentors, William Dean Howells. For Tolstoy and Howells, Christianity implies a doctrine of complicity: if someone witnesses an immoral act and does nothing to stop it, he or she shares responsibility for the consequences of the act. In this sense, the Easterner correctly implicates others in the death of the Swede.

Besides analyzing naturalistic elements and the ending, critics have approached the story as a psychological study. John Berryman reads it as Crane's confrontation with an Oedipal guilt concerning his rejection of his father's religious values and his anxiety that his family would disapprove of his bohemian lifestyle. Scully represents Crane's father; Johnnie is the "reasonable, decent son" that the dutiful side of Crane wants to be; the Swede is the rebellious side; and the gambler, with his respectable demeanor but violent interior, combines both sides. In killing the Swede, Crane subconsciously tries to atone for the guilt he felt in rebelling against family values (*Stephen Crane* 211–14). Those critics who question Berryman's Freudian reading note that Johnnie as a card cheater is anything but decent and reasonable, and the Swede, who "distrusts life and runs to meet and shape his own destiny," is the opposite of Crane, who had "a fatalistic resignation to what happens" (Stallman, "Short Stories" 108). A more broadly based psychological reading is Ronald McFarland's Jungian approach that analyzes archetypal characters and situations, specifically hospitality codes that have existed in culture and literature from the beginning of recorded history. These are the unspoken codes of behavior that an outsider and a community exhibit when first meeting each other. According to McFarland, "The Blue Hotel" dramatizes the breakdown of a civilized code of etiquette. In one way or another, all of the major characters break the code. Scully, for example, plays the role of the gracious host, but his motive is at least pecuniary; Johnnie cheats innocent strangers; and the Swede acts boorishly. Unlike the ancient world of Homer's *Odyssey* in which codes of behavior helped to maintain community, in the modern world of Crane's story they have lost significance.

Chester L. Wolford explores classical allusions in "The Blue Hotel" and argues that the story—indeed, much of Crane's canon—can be understood within the epic tradition. Just as epics often depict the end of a heroic age, "The Blue Hotel" depicts the end of a heroic West in which the Swede is a tragic hero who "sees the world as a place that still holds out the possibility for individual heroism, honesty, and truth" (*Anger* 102). The images, phrasing, and structure of the story echo the classical tradition. For example, the kings and queens, high-valued face cards scattered on the floor of the hotel, remind the reader that the classical tradition recounts stories about noble figures; patronymic phrasing such as "John, son of Scully" (*Prose* 801) and epithets with compound adjectives as in "an old farmer who had whiskers both gray and sandy" (800) are stock diction in epics; and the final section of the story functions like an epilogue in Greek tragedy in which the chorus comments on the action. Although the Swede dies because his vision of the West clashes with one in which Fort Romper will soon be "a met-tro-*pol*-is" with "a line of ilictric street-cars" (807, 806), he is, for Wolford, in the tradition of great tragic heroes like

Achilles in the *Iliad* and Aeneas in the *Aeneid* who fight for noble values but are ultimately defeated by less heroic figures.

Unlike critics who see the action in "The Blue Hotel" as timeless, William Bysshe Stein interprets it as a forerunner of twentieth-century existentialism: "Like Kierkegaard and Kafka Crane finds the absurd in every walk and in every stage of life. It manifests itself in the contradictions of social experience independent of class and position" (182). Although the Easterner's comments at the end about causality, freedom of choice, and moral responsibility suggest a Christian outlook, they are invalid in a chaotic universe. Characters are "hopelessly self-absorbed and ... lost in contemplation of some private vision of [their] personal role in the universe." Scully can think only about hospitality; Johnnie, only about card cheating. The cowboy is full of "bravado"; the Easterner, "intellectual self-reliance." The townspeople focus only on civic pride; the gambler, on self-importance. As a result, "[e]ach individual is pathetically estranged from the world in which he seeks to enact a particular role; for his aspirations and desires are completely uncoordinated with any common goal in life." When the Swede attempts to impose his vision on an absurd, disjointed universe, he is bound to be destroyed by it (173-74). In capturing the classic existential dilemma as propounded by Sartre and Camus—a sense of alienation because of the absurdity of experience—Crane is the most modern of late nineteenth-century authors. This may partly explain Ernest Hemingway's famous quotation about major influences on modern American literature: "The good writers are Henry James, Stephen Crane, and Mark Twain. That's not the order they're good in. There is no order for good writers.... . Crane wrote two fine stories. 'The Open Boat' and 'The Blue Hotel.' The last one is the best" (Hemingway, *Green Hills* 22).

9

The *Commodore* Experience

Crane transformed his near-death experience on the *Commodore* into three accounts: a feature newspaper article titled "Stephen Crane's Own Story" and two short stories: the classic, "The Open Boat" and an adventurous tale, "Flanagan and His Short Filibustering Adventure." *Filibustering* was the name given to the tactic of smuggling arms to the insurgents in Cuba. The word derives from the Spanish word *filibustero*, meaning "freebooter." The boats, which included the *Commodore*, were called "filibusters."

"STEPHEN CRANE'S OWN STORY"

Crane's newspaper account of the *Commodore* experience gives the details surrounding its fateful voyage. The most graphic part of the account is the attempt to rescue men on one of the makeshift rafts. A man on the raft threw a line to the dinghy—which contained Crane, the captain, the oiler, and the cook—with the hope that the dinghy could tow the raft. When this plan failed, the man tried to get to the dinghy, which was only six inches above the water's edge, by pulling in the line. According to Crane, "[h]e had turned into a demon. He was wild, wild as a tiger. He was crouched on this raft and ready to spring. Every muscle of him seemed to be turned into an elastic spring. His eyes were almost white. His face was the face of a lost man reaching upward, and we knew that the weight of his hand on our gunwale doomed us. The cook let go of the line." When the *Commodore* sank, "the rafts were suddenly swallowed by this frightful maw of the ocean" (*Prose* 883). The last two paragraphs of the newspaper article condense a number of details pertaining to the bravery of the captain and the oiler, the capsizing of the dinghy in the breakers, and the oiler's death.

Crane relies on imagery to dramatize the factual details. He creates a sense of ominous foreboding in the opening paragraph: As cargo is loaded onto the ship, its hatch is "like the mouth of a monster ... [during] the feeding time of some legendary creature of the sea" (875). The ship is variously described as a "rubber ball" and a "duck" as it sails; the engine room with its burning coal resembled "the middle kitchen of Hades"; and a lifeboat is so heavy that "[w]e could have pushed a little brick schoolhouse along a corduroy road as easily as we could have moved this boat" (877, 879, 880). Aware of himself as "the writer," Crane creates a sense of immediacy by suddenly supplying details that he "had forgotten to mention" earlier in his account, but he consciously chooses to say nothing about the ordeal on the dinghy after the *Commodore* sinks: "The history of life in an open boat for thirty hours would no doubt be very instructive for the young, but none is to be told here now. For my part I would prefer to tell the story at once, because from it would shine the splendid manhood of Captain Edward Murphy and of William Higgins, the oiler" (883–84).

"THE OPEN BOAT: A TALE INTENDED TO BE AFTER THE FACT, BEING THE EXPERIENCE OF FOUR MEN FROM THE SUNK STEAMER 'COMMODORE'"

BACKGROUND

Following the newspaper account, Crane's immediate impulse was to celebrate the heroism of two of his fellow seamen, but he first needed to make sense of the whole experience before he transformed it into a story. Between mid-January and early February, Crane was back in New York City writing "The Open Boat." Wanting to make sure he had captured the experience completely, he returned to Jacksonville to show it to Captain Murphy. One evening, a fellow journalist who was with Crane and the captain recalled that Crane began to read aloud to the captain something that was evidently in manuscript. He stopped reading to say,

> "Listen, Ed, I want to have this *right*, from your point of view. How does it sound so far?"
> "You've got it, Steve," said the other man. "That is just how it happened, and how we felt. Read me some more of it."

A silence in the alcove and Captain Murphy commented,

> "The Commodore was a rotten old basket of junk, Steve, but I guess I did feel something like that when she went under. How do you wind it up, when poor old Billie was floating face down and all those people came running down to pull us out of the breakers?" [Crane reads the concluding paragraphs of the story.]
> "Do you like it or not, Ed?" asked Stephen Crane.
> "It's good, Steve. Poor old Billie! Too bad he had to drown. He was a damn good oiler." (Paine 168, 170)

ANALYSIS

"The Open Boat" is Crane's most frequently anthologized short story and one of the most famous in world literature. Two of Crane's friends—and important literary figures in their own right—recognized its greatness. As Joseph Conrad wrote, "you—by all the devils—fill the sea-scape. The boat thing is immensely interesting. I don't use the word in its common sense. It is fundamentally interesting to me. Your temperament makes old things new and new things amazing.... The illusions of life come out of your hand without a flaw. It is not life— which nobody wants—it is art—art for which everyone—the abject and the great hanker—mostly without knowing it" (*Correspondence* 315). H. G. Wells considered it Crane's best story because of its "stark power" and its "disciplined and controlled" imagery (130).

In retelling his experience at sea, Crane wanted to do more than simply recount the incident; instead, he explored its social and metaphysical implications. The first sentence, "None of them knew the color of the sky" (*Prose* 885), makes clear that perspective is central to the story. More specifically, the story fluctuates between the point of view of the men in the boat, whose focus is strictly on the "walls of water" and "barbarously abrupt and tall" waves that threaten their survival, and an omniscient author, whose view "from a balcony, [would make] the whole thing … weirdly picturesque" (885, 886). Out of necessity they divide up their duties: the oiler and correspondent row, the cook bails out water from the boat, and the captain, whose arm is broken, controls the tiller. The intensity of the situation is made worse by an argument between the cook and correspondent about the likelihood of rescue, by the vulnerability of a boat that seems no bigger than "a bath-tub," and by the "loud swishing" of a shark moving like "a monstrous knife" near them (885, 900, 901).

When the men believe they will soon be rescued, they smoke cigars, drink from their supply of water, and relax "with an assurance … shining in their eyes" (892). This hope, however, is quickly undercut, for they soon realize that rather than living in an orderly world that can ensure salvation, they are isolated victims floating in an irrational cosmos that is hostile or indifferent to their plight. Angry at his fate, the correspondent complains,

> If I am going to be drowned—if I am going to be drowned—if I am going to be drowned, why, in the name of the seven mad gods who rule the sea, was I allowed to come thus far and contemplate sand and trees? Was I brought here merely to have my nose dragged away as I was about to nibble the sacred cheese of life? It is preposterous. If this old ninny-woman, Fate, cannot do better than this, she should be deprived of the management of men's fortunes. She is an old hen who knows not her intention. If she has decided to drown me, why did she not do it in the beginning and save me all this trouble. The whole affair is absurd. (894)

Considering himself important, the correspondent is upset because he is not allowed to know the rules of life, but he painfully comes to realize, "When it occurs to a man that nature does not regard him as important, and that she feels she would not maim the universe by disposing of him, he at first wishes to throw bricks at the temple, and he hates deeply the fact that there are no bricks and no temples" (902). In an indifferent universe symbolized by a "high cold star" and a tower looking like "a giant, standing with its back to the plight of the ants," there is no spiritual court of appeals to lodge a complaint about unfair treatment, about "the struggles of the individual," about life itself (902, 905).

Despite the bleakness of existence, the men develop a "subtle brotherhood" as they develop a community of trust and concern (890). The correspondent recalls a poem about a dying soldier that he was forced to memorize in school. At the time it meant nothing to him, but now, facing the possibility of his own death, he realizes that literature, here in the form of a poem about comradeship, can help him find some sort of meaning in an indifferent universe. As the dinghy finally gets close to shore, this comradeship is augmented by a bystander who, "like a saint" with "a halo about his head," pulls the exhausted men from the breakers and by a community of people with blankets, clothing, coffee, "and all the remedies sacred to their minds." Sadly, the oiler, ironically the best swimmer, dies before getting to shore. The story ends with peaceful imagery of the night and ocean and a realization that now the four men "felt that they could then be interpreters" (909). Despite their own insignificance in an indifferent universe, they had learned the value of solidarity and compassion.

Crane links "The Open Boat" to "Stephen Crane's Own Story" by alluding to the sinking of the *Commodore* and the loss of seven men in the opening paragraphs: "the stern impression of a scene in the grays of dawn of seven turned faces, and later a stump of a top-mast with a white ball on it that slashed to and fro at the waves, went low and lower, and down" (885–86). Besides the obvious connections between the two pieces, however, there are important differences. Whereas "Stephen Crane's Own Story" focuses primarily on action leading up to and during the sinking, "The Open Boat" raises larger metaphysical questions about the nature of existence and the universe. Crane's need to answer these questions for himself explains why he could write a factual account within days, but "[t]he history of life in an open boat … [could not] be told here now." Crane needed the emotional distance from the facts to avoid the possibility of relying on clichés and melodrama and to organize the details into what is today widely acknowledged as a masterpiece. The harrowing experience remained with him, however, for the rest of his life. On his deathbed, as Cora recalled, "My husbands [*sic*] brain is never at rest. He lives over everything in dreams & talks aloud constantly. It is too awful to hear him try to change places in the 'open boat'!" (*Correspondence* 655–56).

AN EXISTENTIALIST READING OF "THE OPEN BOAT"

Existentialism is a term used to describe one of the most dominant philosophical, religious, and artistic schools of thought in the twentieth century. Developed during and after the Second World War, it has its roots in the writings of Søren Kierkegaard, a nineteenth-century Danish theologian. Because the term has been used so differently by many writers, it is difficult to give it a precise definition. Many of its advocates, however, would agree upon the following tenets: Humans and "things"—for example, nature, the changing of the seasons, cataclysmic events—exist, but there is no inherent reason why they exist, unless we give them meaning. Trying to make sense of why things are the way they are is ultimately an attempt to understand an irrational universe in which facts have no inherent meaning. This frustrating attempt to search for some sort of cosmic order can eventually lead to anxiety, loneliness, and despair. An individual learns to trust only in his or her immediate concrete experience rather than in abstractions such as truth, justice, and honor. In contrast to this nihilistic view of reality is Christian existentialism, which, despite the cries of despair of Job or the preacher's lament that "vanity of vanities; all is vanity" in the Old Testament (Job, Ecclesiastes), accepts through blind faith the existence of some greater order.

One extended passage in "The Open Boat" offers an excellent opportunity to examine existentialism. Because the passage is best understood as a unit, it is reproduced here. The four men have just noticed people on shore:

> "Look! There's a man on the shore!"
> "Where?"
> "There! See 'im? See 'im?"
> "Yes, sure! He's walking along."
> "Now he's stopped. Look! He's facing us!"
> "He's waving at us!"
> "So he is! By thunder!"
> "Ah, now, we're all right! Now we're all right! There'll be a boat out here for us in half an hour."
> "He's going on. He's running. He's going up to that house there."
> The remote beach seemed lower than the sea, and it required a searching glance to discern the little black figure. The captain saw a floating stick and they rowed to it. A bath-towel was by some weird chance in the boat, and, tying this on the stick, the captain waved it. The oarsman did not dare turn his head, so he was obliged to ask questions.
> "What's he doing now?"
> "He's standing still again. He's looking, I think.... There he goes again. Toward the house.... Now he's stopped again."
> "Is he waving at us?"
> "No, not now! he was, though."
> "Look! There comes another man!"
> "He's running."
> "Look at him go, would you."
> "Why, he's on a bicycle. Now he's met the other man. They're both waving at us. Look!"

"There comes something up the beach."

"What the devil is that thing?"

"Why, it looks like a boat."

"Why, certainly it's a boat."

"No, it's on wheels."

"Yes, so it is. Well, that must be the life-boat. They drag them along shore on a wagon."

"That's the life-boat, sure."

"No, by——, it's—it's an omnibus."

"I tell you it's a life-boat."

"It is not! It's an omnibus. I can see it plain. See? One of these big hotel omnibuses."

"By thunder, you're right. It's an omnibus, sure as fate. What do you suppose they are doing with an omnibus? Maybe they are going around collecting the life-crew, hey?"

"That's it, likely. Look! There's a fellow waving a little black flag.

He's standing on the steps of the omnibus. There come those other two fellows. Now they're all talking together. Look at the fellow with the flag. Maybe he ain't waving it."

"That ain't a flag, is it? That's his coat. Why, certainly, that's his coat."

"So it is. It's his coat. He's taken it off and is waving it around his head. But would you look at him swing it."

"Oh, say, there isn't any life-saving station there. That's just a winter resort hotel omnibus that has brought over some of the boarders to see us drown."

"What's that idiot with the coat mean? What's he signaling, anyhow?"

"It looks as if he were trying to tell us to go north. There must be a life-saving station up there."

"No! He thinks we're fishing. Just giving us a merry hand. See? Ah, there, Willie."

"Well, I wish I could make something out of those signals. What do you suppose he means?"

"He don't mean anything. He's just playing."

"Well, if he'd just signal us to try the surf again, or to go to sea and wait, or go north, or go south, or go to hell—there would be some reason in it. But look at him. He just stands there and keeps his coat revolving like a wheel. The ass!"

"There come more people."

"Now there's quite a mob. Look! Isn't that a boat?"

"Where? Oh, I see where you mean. No, that's no boat."

"That fellow is still waving his coat."

"He must think we like to see him do that. Why don't he quit it. It don't mean anything." (*Prose* 895–97)

One notices immediately certain characteristics about the text. There is little expository prose supplying background, description, or commentary; instead, the text is almost pure dialogue. Second, missing are tags like "the correspondent says" identifying the speakers. If one limits the conversation to the oiler and the correspondent, the last two speakers clearly identified in the story before the quoted passage, it is still unclear who is speaking when. Even when the speaker of the question, "'What's he doing now?'" is identified as the oarsman, this person could be either the oiler or the correspondent because each rows at some point. Because the dialogue is spoken without tags, readers want to make sense of the statements by arbitrarily assigning tags to them. But one could look at the same set of "facts"—the actual statements themselves—rearrange the tags so that someone else in the boat says some of the lines, and still have a semblance of meaning.

In addition, there is confusion of what one sees and the significance of it. What first appears to be a lifeboat is an omnibus, and when properly identified, it is misconstrued as a vehicle for "collecting the life-crew." What seems to be a flag is actually a coat being waved by an "idiot" whose attempt to communicate with "signals" merely causes confusion: "'What do you suppose he means?'" Indeed, attempts to "make something out of those signals," to find "some reason" in them, ultimately lead to failure: "'It don't mean anything.'" This is a universe in which things happen by "some weird chance," as the discovery of a "bath-towel" in an open boat. With the absence of cosmic order and the breakdown in communication between the men in the dinghy and the spectators on shore, one has the classic existential dilemma: humans have the freedom to act, but their actions are, as recorded in *Macbeth*, "a tale / Told by an idiot, full of sound and fury, / Signifying nothing" (Shakespeare 5.5.26–28).

In a Darwinian world of the survival of the fittest, the oiler, the strongest swimmer, would survive, and the weakest, the wounded captain, would not. In the final section of the story, however, the narrator allows for the possibility of a Christian existentialist interpretation, for "[t]he race is not to the swift, nor the battle to the strong" (Ecclesiastes 9:11). When the four men seem doomed to die, a rescuer who "magically" appears is their deus ex machina (*Prose* 908). With "a halo about his head ... he [shines] like a saint" who is "naked as a tree in winter." In the death and darkness of winter, he is their tree of life and hope. Once on shore, the four men find literal and spiritual protection in the community of people "and all the remedies sacred to their minds" (909). Despite "disjointed sentences" (887) spoken between the cook and the correspondent as well as the inability to make sense of their immediate experience, the men ultimately form a "subtle brotherhood" that allows them to become "interpreters" (890, 909).

"FLANAGAN AND HIS SHORT FILIBUSTERING ADVENTURE"

Flanagan, who gets involved in filibustering "just for fun, mostly," is captain of the *Foundling,* a ship in "medieval disrepair" with an engine "as whimsical as a gas-meter" (*Prose* 912, 913). After surviving one storm en route to deliver insurgents and munitions to Cuba, the ship encounters another, which leaves a number of the crew and insurgents sick or injured. The ship, however, successfully reaches Cuba and avoids getting captured by a Spanish gunboat. On the return trip to Florida during another storm, the crew is forced to abandon ship in lifeboats when trouble develops in the engine room. In the attempt to reach shore, Flanagan drowns in the surf. As a brief outline of the plot makes clear, there are obvious similarities between this story and the *Commodore* incident: in both, the boats were involved in filibustering, they had engine trouble before sinking, insurgents got seasick, and a crewman drowned in the breakers.

Unlike "The Open Boat," Crane wrote this story hastily because he needed money. Before leaving for Jacksonville in late November 1896, the Bacheller syndicate had given him $700 in Spanish gold as a retainer to cover expenses in Cuba, but he apparently either threw it overboard before getting into the dinghy or lost it in the surf. In March 1897 the publisher S. S. McClure lent him $600–700 in exchange for giving McClure first option on serial publication of his next stories and first option on his next book. Because he was scheduled to sail for England during the same month on his way to report on the Greek-Turkish conflict, he composed "Flanagan and His Short Filibustering Adventure" quickly so that McClure would have at least one story before he left. As a result of the circumstances of composition, the story is, as the title says, essentially an adventure.

Nevertheless, the story is similar to other stories by Crane—for example, "The Five White Mice," "An Episode of War," and "War Memories"—in which an ironic ending seems to undercut the attempt of a character to make sense of his experience. Flanagan's assignment as captain is an initiation into filibustering. He is successful in getting the insurgents and munitions to Cuba and in avoiding getting captured by the Spanish, but his death prevents him from benefiting as a result of the experience. His attempt to help the rebellion against Spanish occupation of Cuba is made more empty by the fact that the people on shore are more interested in the prospect of lifeboats landing as entertainment rather than as an occasion for rescue and comfort, and when Flanagan's corpse washes ashore, it is met with the indifference of spectators more concerned about getting their shoes and clothing wet in the surf. As the narrator laments in the last line of the story, "[t]he expedition of the *Foundling* will never be historic" (925). Flanagan's heroic effort will remain forgotten in the annals of history.

Yet at the same time, as is so often the case with Crane's work, the ending is filled with irony, and the narrator memorializes Flanagan in the annals of literature. As in "The Blue Hotel," in which the last section is an ironic commentary on the penultimate section, the ending of "Flanagan and His Short Filibustering Adventure" has two parts marked by a break in the text. In the first part, in which the ship is damaged, there is a calm dignity as the captain "took control of himself suddenly," and the men "submitted" to his orders because he had developed grace under pressure and had become a true leader: "The situation simply required a Voice." Having grown from his fateful experience on the *Foundling,* "he understood doom and its weight and complexion." As the ship sinks, there is no "pageantry of uproar," only the tears and anger of the captain (924).

In contrast to the "quiet death" of the ship, which "shifted and settled as calmly as an animal curls down in the bush grass … without pageantry of uproar" (924), in the second part there is the world of pageantry "at the Imperial Inn," where the plashing of water in a courtyard fountain, the artificially colored "rose light upon the gleaming leaves," and music "like the melodies in dreams" (924, 925) create a romanticized view of reality that is "destroyed" with news of the shipwreck. The worlds of romance and reality are juxtaposed when the narrator uses the same verb to depict the final scene: "From the throng of charming women floated the perfume of many flowers. Later there floated to them a body with a calm face of an Irish type" (925). From the point of view of the partygoers at the "charming dance" (924), they feel justified in retreating to "the shelter of the great hotel" (925) and forgetting about the shipwreck; however, there is a different perspective from the point of view of the narrator. Just as Crane had juxtaposed two opposing perspectives in "The Open

Boat"—the inability of the four men in the dinghy to know "the color of the sky" and a perspective of their dilemma "[v]iewed from a balcony"—so too does he here (885, 886). Observing the action of the partygoers is "a mocking-bird" "[h]igh on some balcony" (924)— certainly an appropriate metaphor for a disdainful narrator who exposes their moral callousness. While condemning them for deserting the orphans of the *Foundling,* the narrator, like a good parent, has rescued them through the annals of fiction.

10

Poetry

THE BLACK RIDERS AND OTHER LINES

Stephen Crane's first book of poems, *The Black Riders and Other Lines,* was published by Copeland & Day in 1895. Although Crane began writing poetry when he was eight years old, it is unclear at what point as an adult that he started to think seriously about continuing to do so. Sometime in 1893, William Dean Howells read some of Emily Dickinson's poetry to Crane, who was impressed with it. Shortly after this incident, Crane showed a friend 30 poems and claimed to have written them in three days. In early 1894 Crane showed another friend, Corwin Knapp Linson, several poems and asked for comments:

> "What do you think I have been doing, CK?"
> When a question is unanswerable one merely waits. Responding to my inquiring gaze, he laid the sheets on my drawing as if to say, "That, just now, is of minor importance." I read the topmost script….
> I became conscious of an uneasy waiting—then a swift challenge. "What do you think?"
> "I haven't had time to think! I'm seeing pictures."
> "What do you mean?"
> "Just what I said. They make me see pictures. How did you think of them?"
> A finger passed across his forehead, "They came, and I wrote them, that's all." … I confessed that their newness of form, their disregard of

the usual puzzled me—"but that's their value, after all, Steve. I'm glad they're not Whitman. I thought at first they might be." He laughed.

"That's all right, CK. If you can see them like that it's all I want." And he broke into a little chant. (*My Stephen Crane* 48-50)

The following month, he showed poems to Hamlin Garland and asked the same question:

I read this [the poem "God fashioned the ship of the world carefully"] with delight and amazement. I rushed through the others, some thirty in all, with growing wonder. I could not believe they were the work of the pale, reticent boy moving restlessly about the room.

"Have you any more?" I asked.

"I've got five or six all in a little row up here," he quaintly replied, pointing to his temple. "That's the way they come—in little rows, all made up, ready to be put down on paper."

"When did you write these?"

"Oh! I've been writing five or six every day. I wrote nine yesterday. I wanted to write some more last night, but those 'Indians' [Crane's nickname for his roommates] wouldn't let me do it. They howled over the other verses so loud they nearly cracked my ears. You see, we all live in a box together and I've no place to write, except right in the general squabble. They think my lines are funny. They make a circus of me." ("Soldier of Fortune" 16)

As these reminiscences suggest, Crane's verse was distinctive; he referred to it as "lines" rather than poems; and he could apparently write them quickly, although there is no real evidence to support this belief. Most of the lines in *The Black Riders* are first-person accounts that depict dramatic conflict. Written in free verse, they are short and pithy and explore cosmic issues about the nature of God and existence. In contrast to much of the poetry written at the time, which was thoroughly conventional and genteel, Crane's verse was stark and iconoclastic. By calling them lines, he clearly was proclaiming that he was not a poet in the traditional sense of the word. As Daniel Hoffman has observed, "[h]is unmetered, unrhymed lines appeared shocking, as did his manhandling of conventional religious themes. His 'lines' set their first readers' teeth on edge: they were attacked for their apparent barbarism, their want of art, the author's nerve in trying to pass off as poetry such 'disjointed effusions'" ("Many Red Devils" 590).

At the same time, the lines record an internal monologue in which Crane confronts the spiritual beliefs of his ancestors. Though he rejected the image of an unforgiving, wrathful God as portrayed by the Revs. George and Jesse Peck, his maternal grandfather and maternal great-uncle, and most likely by his father, Rev. Jonathan Townley Crane, it haunted him throughout his life. As the American poet Amy Lowell noticed, "Crane was so steeped in the religion in which he was brought up that he could not get it out of his head. He disbelieved it and he hated it, but he could not free himself from it" (xix). Throughout *The Black Riders* Crane contrasts his family's image of an angry Old Testament God with a forgiving New Testament One more accepting of humanity's fallibility.

The title poem of *The Black Riders* abruptly introduces an apocalyptic vision of a universe steeped in sin:

> Black riders came from the sea.
> There was clang and clang of spear and shield,
> And clash and clash of hoof and heel,
> Wild shouts and the wave of hair
> In the rush upon the wind:
> Thus the ride of Sin. (*Prose* 1299)

Despite contemporary claims that Crane's verse lacked artistry, this example demonstrates how alliteration and onomatopoeia in phrases such as "clang and clang," "clash and clash," and "rush … ride" intensify the impact of a poem in which the identification of the "Black riders" is not clarified until the last word.

Throughout *The Black Riders* humanity is forced to survive on its own. Although "God fashioned the ship of the world carefully," He did not include a rudder. Before launching the ship, He got distracted and the ship slipped away

> So that, forever rudderless, it went upon the seas
> Going ridiculous voyages,
> Making quaint progress,
> Turning as with serious purpose
> Before stupid winds. (1300–01)

Any attempt to plead for help is met with anger and derision by a God who is "Fat with rage and puffing" in one poem and "Blustering … [and] Stamping across the sky / With loud swagger" in another (1317, 1318). The narrator even questions whether or not God exists at all:

> If I should find nothing there
> But a vast blue,

Echoless, ignorant—
What then? (1323)

In "God lay dead in Heaven," "monsters ... Wrangled over the world," and humanity was at the mercy of "the jaws of the final beast" (1324). Like the depiction of God, nature is perceived as angry or indifferent in a setting of "direful thickets" and "snow, ice, burning sand" (1304, 1305).

Given the hostile universe humanity finds itself in, the question becomes whether or not one can find meaning in life. When "A learned man" claims to know the path to truth, the narrator is "overjoyed" but soon becomes despondent when the man cries out, "'I am lost'" (1305). When another person claims to have found ultimate truth after "pursuing the horizon," he calls the narrator a liar for questioning his own certainty (1306). In another poem he contrasts two perspectives and associates those who claim certainty with institutionalized religion:

> "Truth," said a traveller,
> "Is a rock, a mighty fortress;
> Often have I been to it,
> Even to its highest tower,
> From whence the world looks black."
>
> "Truth," said a traveller,
> "Is a breath, a wind,
> A shadow, a phantom;
> Long have I pursued it,
> But never have I touched
> The hem of its garment."
>
> And I believed the second traveller;
> For truth was to me
> A breath, a wind,
> A shadow, a phantom,
> And never had I touched
> The hem of its garment. (1308)

In the first stanza a traveler believes that truth is as hard and visible as "a rock" or "mighty fortress," which also alludes to a line in Psalm 18 in the Old Testament: "The Lord is my rock, my fortress"; but he concludes pessimistically that "the world looks black." In contrast, however, is a traveler who views truth as fleeting and ethereal as "breath," "wind," "shadow," or "phantom." Whereas the first traveler proclaims arrogantly his knowledge of truth—"Often have I been to it," the second humbly acknowledges his own uncertainty about absolute truth—"never have I touched / The hem of its garment." Unlike the diseased woman who touched the hem of Jesus's garment so that her faith might cure her (Matthew 9:20–22), the narrator and the "second traveller" have only their own experience on which to build their faith. Crane objected not to the idea of religious faith but to the way that society had created a "fortress" of institutionalized religion based on hypocrisy, intolerance, and dogmatism. In another poem, when a minister, "A man in strange black garb," meets a divine "radiant form," "the spirit knew him not" (*Prose* 1320), and when angels see "Little black streams of people" entering "a fat church," they are confused as to why these people went there (1309).

Despite cries of doubt and despair in *The Black Riders,* the narrator never ultimately becomes a nihilist, for there are moments in which "The voice of God whispers in the heart / So softly" and "The God of his inner thoughts … with infinite comprehension [says] 'My poor child!'" (1312, 1317). Crane believed in what Ralph Waldo Emerson called the need for each individual to establish an "original relation to the universe" (27). In a larger sense, Crane was reflecting a major characteristic in American literature, what Philip Rahv has called the "cult of experience." Whether it was Thoreau's living by Walden Pond, Twain's reminiscing about the Mississippi River, or Whitman's writing his "Song of Myself," American writers have valued the importance of individual experience.

CONTEMPORARY RECEPTION

When *The Black Riders* was published by the avant-garde firm Copeland and Day, it created a stir because of its contents and unconventional appearance. The layout of the title page was striking. The title was printed in all capital letters, and Crane's first name was hyphenated: "THE BLACK RIDERS AND/OTHER LINES BY STE-/PHEN CRANE." Beneath the title was a large block of white space, followed at the bottom of the page by "BOSTON COPELAND AND DAY MDCCCXCV." Each poem was printed separately in all capital letters at the top of a page, with the rest of the page left blank.

Critics disagreed widely on the merits of the poems. Harry Thurston Peck drew national attention to *The Black Riders* in the *Bookman,* an influential literary magazine that reflected and helped to shape the reading interests of Americans. Peck's decision to write a feature article on Crane and to review his recently published collection of poems in the

Bookman reveals the impact that the young author had already made on literary America. Peck compared Crane to Walt Whitman and Aubrey Beardsley, the English illustrator whose ornate, elegant drawings made him a central figure in the art nouveau movement in the 1890s:

> Mr. Crane is the Aubrey Beardsley of poetry. When one first takes up his little book of verse and notes the quite too Beardsleyesque splash of black upon its staring white boards, and then on opening it discovers that the "lines" are printed wholly in capitals, and that they are unrhymed and destitute of what most poets regard as rhythm, the general impression is of a writer who is bidding for renown wholly on the basis of his eccentricity. But just as Mr. Beardsley with all his absurdities is none the less a master of black and white, so Mr. Crane is a true poet whose verse, long after the eccentricity of its form has worn off, fascinates us and forbids us to lay the volume down until the last line has been read. Even in the most fantastic of his conceits there are readily to be found a thought and a meaning. In fact, if Walt Whitman had been caught young and subjected to aesthetic influences, it is likely that he would have mellowed his barbaric yawp to some such note as that which sounds in the poems that are now before us. (254)

Not everyone, however, appreciated the book. In response to Peck, a reviewer in *Munsey's Magazine* dismissed it as "slovenly work" that revealed Crane's ignorance of "the mechanical secrets of his trade" and asked a rhetorical question: "Is this poetry?" (Weatherford 66, 67). The *Chicago Daily Inter-Ocean* quipped that "[t]he most remarkable thing about this neatly printed little volume is the amount of blank paper—six, eight, and ten lines crowd the bulk of the pages. But after reading, you may well be glad that it is so. There is not a line of poetry from the opening to the closing page. Whitman's 'Leaves of Grass' were luminous in comparison. Poetic lunacy would be a better name for the book" (Ferrara and Dossett 168).

Crane's distinctive poetic style prompted the writing of a number of parodies, called *stephencranelets* by Crane's friend Post Wheeler (Wheeler and Rives 100–01). One such parody appeared in *The Philistine: A Periodical of Protest,* an iconoclastic magazine that enjoyed mocking established literary figures:

AFTER THE MANNER OF MR. STEAMIN' STORK.

> I saw a man making a fool of himself;
> He was writing a poem,
> Scratch, scratch, scratch, went his pen,

"Go 'way, Man," says I; "you can't do it."
He picked up a handful of red devils and
Threw them at my head.
"You infernal liar," he howled,
"I can write poetry with my toes!"
I was disquieted. I turned and
Ran like a Blue Streak for the Horizon,
Yelling Bloody Murder.
When I got there I
Bit a piece out of it
And lay down on my stomach and
Thought.
And breathed hard. (*Log* 136–37)

Like caricature in a political cartoon, parody humorously draws atten-tion to a person, his or her thoughts, or writing style. Though a parody can be a flattering tribute to an author or a harshly satirical look at his style, one thing is clear: only someone who is having an impact is worth parodying. Whether or not people liked *The Black Riders and Other Lines,* they were aware that America was hearing a new poetic voice.

WAR IS KIND

Unlike *The Black Riders and Other Lines, War Is Kind* is more a collection of diverse poems than a stylistically and thematically coher-ent work for three reasons: first, the poems were written over a span of several years; second, more than half of them were published separately in magazines first; and third, though two-thirds of the poems are in free verse, others rely on more traditional patterns of poetry. Before going to Cuba in 1898, Crane began planning the collection and completed it in Havana in fall of that year. The book was published in 1899.

Crane further explores the plight of humanity as depicted in *The Black Riders.* In "In the Night," a voice prays to the "Master that movest the wind with a finger" so "that we may run swiftly across the world / To huddle in worship at Thy feet" and "may sing Thy good-ness to the sun," but there is no response (*Prose* 1333, 1334). In "A slant of sun on dull brown walls," the narrator is more desperate as he cries out in "cluttered incoherency," "O God, save us!" (1332). If God does respond, His answer is bleak and cryptic:

"Have you ever made a just man?"
"Oh, I have made three," answered God,

"But two of them are dead,
And the third—
Listen! Listen!
And you will hear the thud of his defeat." (1327)

Hoping to find the meaning of life elsewhere, the narrator turns to nature, only to discover silence or indifference. Crane's most famous poem sums up the human condition:

A man said to the universe:
"Sir, I exist!"
"However," replied the universe,
"The fact has not created in me
A sense of obligation." (1335)

Besides poems depicting humanity's spiritual isolation in an indifferent world, others in *War Is Kind* are social commentary on contemporary issues. In the title poem, a maiden, a child, and a mother who have lost a loved one in battle are told in a bitterly ironic statement, "Do not weep. / War is kind" (1324). In "A newspaper is a collection of half-injustices," Crane criticizes yellow journalism, in which "A newspaper is a court / Where every one is kindly and unfairly tried / By a squalor of honest men" and in which sales are a measure of success: "a market / Where wisdom sells its freedom" (1330-31). The lust for wealth and economic power is satirized in "The impact of a dollar upon the heart" and "The successful man has thrust himself" in which millionaires are "Slimed with victories over the lesser" (1335, 1333).

War Is Kind ends with 10 effusively sentimental love poems dealing with a man's suspicion about the loyalty of his lover. Whether or not the poems are autobiographical has been debated. The first five poems had been completed by December 1896 or early 1897, and the other five were written or revised in fall 1898, suggesting that they may deal with not just one lover. Although the poems are trite by a reader's standards, they reflect a tortured soul confused about his own emotions.

CONTEMPORARY RECEPTION

The publication of *War Is Kind* was generally received unfavorably. In addition, reviewers criticized Will Bradley's art nouveau illustrations accompanying the poems and the publisher's choice of gray cartridge paper for the printing of the book. Whereas one critic admired Crane's prose in *The Red Badge of Courage,* which "rises almost to the level of epic song at times," as well as the epigrams in *War Is Kind,* which "are obviously prose, nothing more," he read Crane's new book "with woeful disappointment" (Underwood 466, 467). As the title of one review, "Mr. Crane's Crazyquilting," makes clear, another critic dismissed the book as a confusing mess: "What manner of joke Stephen Crane and his illustrator, Will Bradley, had in mind when they got up their new book has not leaked out" (Chelifer 26). Willa Cather, who would later become one of America's leading novelists, considered the book an embarrassment: "This truly remarkable book is printed on dirty gray blotting paper, on each page of which is a mere dot of print over a large I of vacancy. There are seldom more than ten lines on a page, and it would be better if most of those lines were not there at all. Either Mr. Crane is insulting the public or insulting himself, or he has developed a case of atavism and is chattering the primeval nonsense of the apes. His *Black Riders,* uneven as it was, was a casket of polished masterpieces when compared with *War Is Kind*" (Curtin 700).

Ironically, a little more than a decade after Crane's death, critics began viewing his poetry as a forerunner of the imagist movement in the early part of the twentieth century. The American leaders of the movement included Edith Wyatt, Carl Sandburg, and Amy Lowell. Among their beliefs was a desire to write poetry that relied on a specific image at a particular moment, that used common language but avoided clichés, and that suggested rather than articulated the meaning of the poem. Like Crane, they rebelled against the traditional conventions of poetry. Wyatt considered Crane a closer adherent to the principles of Imagism than the Imagists themselves. Lowell's insights about Crane's poetry set the direction for critical analysis of it in the twentieth century.

Sandburg acknowledged his appreciation of Crane—and another influence on the imagists, Emily Dickinson—in his poetry and correspondence. He thanked both in his poem "Letters to Dead Imagists":

Emily Dickinson:

> You gave us the bumble bee who has a soul,
> The everlasting traveler among the hollyhocks,
> And how God plays around a back yard garden.

Stevie Crane:

> War is kind and we never knew the kindness of war till you came;
> Nor the black riders and clashes of spear and shield out of the sea,
> Nor the mumblings and shots that rise from dreams on call.

(Sandburg, Complete Poems 73)

Later he quipped how he, Crane, and Dickinson were misunderstood as poets:

> I wrote poems ... [and] sent them to two editors who rejected them right off. I read those letters of rejection years later and I agreed with those editors. They told me to try them again as they saw signs of hope in me. And I studied about it. I showed a sheaf of the rejected poems to three well-read persons for whose opinions I had respect. In this sheaf I inserted two free verse poems from Stephen Crane's *Black Riders* and one from Emily Dickinson. And two of the well-read persons agreed with the editors in rejecting ALL of the poems. They threw Crane and Emily Dickinson into the discard along with Sandburg. The third judge, a teacher of English, said the two poems of Crane deserved to be printed. I didn't tell them I had slipped three jokers into the deck but I learned you can't trust the judgment of good friends. (Sandburg, *Ever the Winds of Chance* 146-47)

Since the imagist movement, Crane's poems—or "lines" as he preferred to call them—have received occasional attention. A major American poet, John Berryman, has called "War Is Kind" "one of the major lyrics of the century in America" and viewed Crane as "the important American poet between Walt Whitman and Emily Dickinson on one side, and his tardy-developing contemporaries Edwin Arlington Robinson and Robert Frost with Ezra Pound on the other" (Berryman, *Stephen Crane* 271, 269).

Crane realized that his poetry was controversial. When *The Black Riders* was published, he privately admitted that he "was getting very ably laughed at" (*Correspondence* 187), though he preferred it over *The Red Badge* because it was "the more ambitious effort. In it I aim to give my ideas of life as a whole, so far as I know it, and the latter is a mere episode,—an amplification" (231). It is perhaps fitting, therefore, that posterity has given preference to his wish, for his tombstone reads, "Stephen Crane / Poet—Author / 1871-1900."

A NEW CRITICAL READING OF THE POETRY

Shortly before and following World War II, a new way of interpreting literature called New Criticism became popular. As the name suggests, its adherents advocated a change in the way that literature is analyzed. Critics have generally always allowed for the possibility that information about an author's biography and the period in which he or she wrote can be useful in understanding a work of literature. Although not discounting this information, New Critics saw it as background information extrinsic to the work itself. A work of art should be treated as a self-contained object apart from anything else. Knowing who wrote a work, when it was written, and what was happening in society at the time are ultimately immaterial, New Critics argued, because the object is timeless and contains its meaning within itself.

New Critics also believed that the language of literature differed from the language of science and was a valid kind of knowledge. To get to this knowledge—the meaning of the work—New Critics developed a way to do a "close reading" of a text, sometimes called by the French expression *explication de texte*, that focused on the key elements of literature—plot, character, setting, language, symbol, and point of view. In doing so, they analyzed the literary form of the work; hence, they are sometimes called Formalist Critics and their theory has been called the Objective Theory of Art. No other method of literary analysis has had as much influence in the twentieth century as New Criticism.

New Critics often used the following terms in their analyses:

1. *tension*—at first the details of a work may seem disconnected, but ultimately a good work is unified, often through irony or paradox.
2. *intentional fallacy*—it is a mistake to believe that a work can be explained by knowing what an author intended to say when he or she wrote.
3. *affective fallacy*—similarly, it is a mistake to believe that a work can be explained by its effect on a reader. Doing so confuses the work and its impact, in other words, what it is versus what it does. Although readers may be interested in how they *feel* about literature, this has nothing to do with *understanding* the work itself.
4. *form*—a work has parts that fit together to create some sort of form. In poetry, one might talk about the form of the line or stanza; in fiction, the form of a paragraph or chapter; and in drama, the form of a scene or act.

5. *objective correlative*—first used by T. S. Eliot, the phrase refers to the way an author uses a pattern of things, events, or situations to communicate a feeling without directly expressing it.

In analyzing Crane's poetry, a New Critic is interested in patterns within and between poems. For example, 30 of the 68 poems in *The Black Riders* and 17 of the 27 in *War Is Kind* present a confrontation. In *The Black Riders,* 14 poems deal directly with a man searching for truth and in 13 exploring the nature of God. In 23 of the poems the man is considered a fool. Similarly, the use of the words *black* or *blackness* occur 25 times; *little,* 52 times; *God, godly, gods,* 89 times, with other words often repeated as well. If one finds these patterns, however, the question is, what do they help readers understand about the meaning of a poem?

An analysis of the following poem will demonstrate how New Criticism is applied to the study of literature:

> I explain the silvered passing of a ship at night
> The sweep of each sad lost wave,
> The dwindling boom of the steel thing's striving
> The little cry of a man to a man
> A shadow falling across the greyer night
> And the sinking of the small star.
> Then the waste, the far waste of waters,
> And the soft lashing of black waves
> For long and in loneliness.
> Remember, thou, oh ship of love
> Thou leavest a far waste of waters
> And the soft lashing of black waves
> For long and in loneliness.

(*Prose* 1328)

The setting is nighttime at sea when two ships are passing each other. One sailor calls to another, in all likelihood as a gesture of momentary friendship. The word *cry,* however, is a pun, for it refers not only to a man's yelling to be heard but also to a tearful lament. The second stanza suggests why he is sad—he has been lonely for a long time, and something has been wasted—but the lines raise more questions than they answer.

By essentially repeating the lines in the third stanza but adding a fourth line, the last stanza puts the rest of the poem into a context. The ship is a metaphor for the fleeting experience of love. Like passing ships in the night, lovers drift past each other. The point of view of this particular lover, the "I" in the poem, is largely negative, for the end of a relationship has left him only with "waste" and a sense of cosmic isolation. Stylistic techniques reinforce this theme:

1. *Personification* is the attribution of human characteristics to animals, nature, and ideas. When the waves are depicted as "sad," there is a sense that nature feels the loss that love can bring.

2. *Alliteration* is the repetition of vowel or consonant sounds at the beginning of juxtaposed words. The poem relies heavily on three sounds: *s* in "silvered passing," "ship," "sweep," "sad lost," "steel thing's striving," "shadow," "sinking," "small star," "soft"; *w* in "waste," "waste of waters," "waves"; and *l* in "little," "lashing," "long and in loneliness." Unity of sound created by repetition is a way to reinforce unity of theme.

3. A *foot* is the unit of rhythm in poetry. This poem uses a trochaic foot, which consists of an accented syllable followed by an unaccented one. In the following words—"passing," "dwindling," "striving," "falling," "sinking," "lashing"—the stress is on the first syllable. As one reads the words, the voice drops as it reaches the second syllable. The falling sound reiterates the sense of the ending or falling off of a relationship.

4. *Onomatopoeia* is the use of a word that by its sound suggests its meaning. One hears the "boom" of a ship traveling through water, but the adjective "dwindling," with its trochaic foot, moves the sound toward silence.

The whole poem is thus an extended metaphor about love that is set up as a paradox. The first stanza is a declarative sentence with the verb *explain*, which means to clarify in a logical way. Metaphor, however, does not rely on directness and logic; instead, it implies a connection between two things, love and a ship in this instance, that are not logically connected. Paradoxically, the tension between two modes of presentation—the directness of a rational explanation versus the imaginative reconstruction of a point of view relying as much on sound as it does on sense—creates a unified poem.

Other kinds of critics would look at the same poem differently. A biographical critic, for example, would point out that the poem seems to have a deep personal connection for Stephen Crane. The poem was first published in October 1896. By early December he had fallen in love with Cora Ethel Stewart, the woman with whom he would spend the rest of his life.[1] On December 4 he wrote her an inscription about the ephemeral nature of relationships:

To C.E.S.

> Brevity is an element
> that enters importantly
> into all pleasures of
> life and this is
> what makes pleasure sad
> and so there is no
> pleasure but only sadness.
> Stephen Crane
> Jacksonville, Fla

Nov [December] 4th, 1896. (*Correspondence* 269–70)

The following month he wrote another inscription, which paraphrases "I explain the silvered passing of a ship at night":

To C.E.S.

> Love comes like the tall
> swift shadow of a ship at
> night. There is for a mom-
> ent, the music of the water's
> turmoil, a bell, perhaps, a man's shout,
> a row of gleaming yellow lights. Then the
> slow sinking of this mystic
> shape. Then silence and a
> bitter silence—the silence
> of the sea at night.
> Stephen Crane

(*Correspondence* 279–80)

Between the writing of the two inscriptions, Crane had his near-death experience following the sinking of the *Commodore*. If anything, the experience taught him the fragility and mutability of life, which, only months earlier, he had written about in his poem. His two inscriptions, inspired by the poem, are his way of telling Cora about the likely transient nature of their newly found love.

For the New Critic, this interpretation is fraught with problems because it commits the "intentional fallacy." It tries to reconstruct

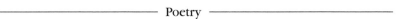
what Crane was thinking about and intending to do in a historical setting different from ours more than 100 years ago. It is safer to treat the poem as a timeless object whose meaning exists internally.

NOTE

1. Different versions of Cora's name can cause confusion. She was born Cora Ethel Eaton Howorth. After a short-lived marriage to Thomas Vinton Murphy, she married an English aristocrat, Captain Donald William Stewart. When Crane met Cora in late 1896, she was estranged from Stewart and was using the name Cora Taylor while operating the Hotel de Dream. In the following two inscriptions, Crane uses the initials of her married name.

11

Tales of Whilomville

Starting in summer 1897 Crane began writing a series of 15 stories about an imaginary town named Whilomville based on his boyhood in Port Jervis, New York. Crane used the archaic word *whilom,* which means "formerly," to suggest stories about the past or "once upon a time." In all likelihood Crane was familiar with the word as a child because several of his relatives organized a fife and drum corps named the "Whilom drum corps" that performed at family reunions (J. K. Peck in Brown and Hernlund 118). Thirteen of the 15 stories focus primarily on children; the other two deal mainly with adults. With the exception of the novella "The Monster," the tone is often ironic and humorous, with elements of the kind of idyllic lifestyle found in *The Adventures of Tom Sawyer,* though there are hints of more serious issues dealing with race, religion, and social identity.

"THE MONSTER"

"The Monster," one of Crane's lesser-known masterpieces and the first Whilomville story written, was published in *Harper's New Monthly Magazine* in 1898 and reappeared—along with "The Blue Hotel" and another Whilomville story, "His New Mittens"—in *The Monster and Other Stories* in 1899. It is unlike the other stories in several ways. It is one of the two stories that focus on adults, and at more than 21,000 words it is considerably longer than any of the others. It depicts Whilomville as a growing city with a theater, fire companies, and electric street cars rather than as a sleepy little town, and it deals directly and disturbingly with complex social issues that are at the heart of America's cultural identity.

The story focuses on Dr. Trescott; his son, Jimmie; and his hostler, Henry Johnson. The action is fairly peaceful until one day, while the doctor is returning from visiting sick patients, his house catches on fire. Aware that Jimmie is stranded in the house, Henry rushes in to save him. On his way out through the fire and smoke, Henry falls in the doctor's laboratory and hits his head. An overheated jar on a table breaks, and liquid chemicals drip onto his "upturned face" and burn it away (*Prose* 406). About the same time, Trescott arrives, runs into the house, and rescues his son. Another man saves Henry and lays the "thing ... on the grass" (408). When the local newspaper mistakenly reports that Henry has died, the townspeople pay "a reverent attention to the memory of this hostler. In the breasts of many people was the regret that they had not known enough to give him a hand and a lift when he was alive, and they judged themselves stupid and ungenerous for this failure." The paper prints an editorial eulogizing him and an account by a fire chief describing Henry's heroism; Henry's friend Miss Bella Farragut unexpectedly announces that she was engaged to him; and his name "became suddenly the title of a saint to the little boys" (412).

When the townspeople discover that Dr. Trescott had saved Henry's life, their attitude toward the hostler changes completely. Though Henry is alive, the chemicals burned off his face; left him with only one eye, which lacks an eyelid; and destroyed part of his brain. Though harmless, he is a monster in the eyes of the town. When Henry's presence continues to scare adults and children, a group of leading citizens confront the doctor about his "questionable charity" toward Henry (413). Concluding that he can no longer house Johnson, Trescott removes him from the community by paying Alek Williams, a black man who lives outside town, to care for him, but when Johnson's presence frightens Alek's family and when "[p]lenty cul'd people folks up my way say it is a devil" (419), Alek refuses to care for Henry unless he can get more money. Before this can happen, however, Henry escapes back to town but is soon put in jail. Again, a group of citizens speak with Trescott about the crisis and offer to arrange for Henry to be put away on "a little no-good farm" or "a public institution" (446), but the doctor, even though his medical practice has suffered miserably, still believes that he should personally care for Henry. Soon thereafter, he becomes painfully aware of the consequences of his actions when he returns home one day to find his wife crying. Though she has planned a tea party, only one of her friends shows up for it. The story ends with the Trescott family as socially isolated as Henry Johnson.

ANALYSIS

"The Monster" is one of Crane's richest stories in terms of theme and symbol. When Crane outlined the story to Joseph Conrad, Conrad responded, "[t]he damned story has been haunting me ever since. I think it must be fine. It's a subject for you" (*Correspondence* 328). From the outset, the story created a considerable amount of controversy. In a review of the book publication of the story in *The Monster and Other Stories,* Julian Hawthorne, Nathaniel Hawthorne's son, condemned it as

> an outrage on art and humanity; and the splendid descriptive ability of the author, his vividness and veracity, only render it more flagrant. Something is fundamentally out of gear in a mind that can reconcile itself to such a performance.... Of constructive ability he shows not a vestige. His outfit for literary purposes consists of a microscopic eye, and a keen sense of the queer, the bizarre, the morbid. His minute analysis produces nothing. He is anything but an artist. (Weatherford 260–61)

William Dean Howells, however, considered it the greatest American short story (Stallman, *Biography* 334), and in the twentieth century, Ralph Ellison, the American author whose novel *Invisible Man* (1952) portrays another "faceless" African American in a white society, commented that between Twain and Faulkner "no artist of Crane's caliber looked so steadily at the wholeness of American life and discovered such far-reaching symbolic equivalents for its unceasing state of civil war. Crane's work remains fresh today because he was a great artist, but perhaps he became a great artist because under conditions of pressure and panic he stuck to his guns" (24).

At the heart of the story is Dr. Trescott's controversial decision to avoid euthanasia and save Henry Johnson. As the judge admonishes the doctor, the decision has enormous consequences: "'He will be your creation, you understand. He is purely your creation. Nature has very evidently given him up. He is dead. You are restoring him to life. You are making him, and he will be a monster, and with no mind.'" For the townspeople, the matter is simple: Henry should have been allowed to die, but if he lives, he should be isolated from the community because he is now a monster. One might argue that a doctor's Hippocratic oath is reason enough to preserve life, but the issue is more complicated, for Trescott repeatedly implies that his sense of professional obligation to Henry is at least partly because "'[h]e saved my boy's life'" (*Prose* 414). In addition, the judge's statement that Trescott is "restoring him to life" implies that he has been acting like the arrogant doctor who creates a monster in *Frankenstein* or like Jesus when He brings Lazarus back to life. Crane suggests this Godlike ability of Trescott by naming the spokesperson for the group of concerned citizens John Twelve, an allusion to chapter 12 of the Gospel of John, which contains part of the story about Lazarus.

The implications of the doctor's decision to preserve Henry's life are foreshadowed in the opening section of the story. Jimmie Trescott is playing train with his cart when he accidentally destroys a flower. Although he tries to resuscitate it, he "could do no reparation" (391). When his father discovers the infraction, he exiles his son, who "had not faced his father," from the garden (392). The imagery of destruction/resuscitation, facelessness, and banishment is clear. Henry's facelessness will lead to his and the Trescott family's banishment. The doctor soon loses patients; the next-door neighbors, the Hannigan family, plan to move out; and local residents become hostile as they develop a mob mentality toward him and Henry. When Henry runs loose through Whilomville, people stone him, though as the chief of police tries to explain, "nobody really wanted to hit him, but you know how a crowd gets" (431). Indeed, Trescott does, for he fully realizes that he has created for himself "an utterly new challenge in the night of the jungle" (441).

But at the same time, even if Trescott made the wrong decision in hindsight, there is the question of the town's abhorrence toward Henry. The town's position is clearly stated in a barbershop scene in which a customer asks, "'Well, what makes [Henry] so terrible?'" to which the reply is "'Because he hasn't got any face'" (423). What makes him monstrous, in other words, is his appearance. Because of a badly scarred face and an eye that never shuts close, townspeople are constantly mortified by his presence. As the police chief reports to Dr. Trescott, "'First thing he did was to break up a children's party at Page's. Then he went to Watermelon Alley. Whoo! He stampeded the whole outfit. Men, women, and children running pell-mell, and yelling. They say one old woman broke her leg, or something, shinning over a fence. Then he went right out on the main street, and an

Irish girl threw a fit, and there was a sort of riot'" (431). When Henry comes to live with the Williams family, Mrs. Williams "almost achieved a back somersault," and her children "made simultaneous plunge for a position behind the stove, and formed a wailing heap" (417).

The fact that Henry's presence has disrupted the peaceful social fabric of Whilomville raises another question: Who is the monster? Of course, in the eyes of the community the answer is simple: Henry Johnson. But in the eyes of the reader, the community's reaction is monstrous. Throughout the story the central metaphor is sight, and the dominant theme is misperception. The town constantly misreads the truth about Henry, whether it be when a barber concludes that, based solely on Henry's dress and demeanor, he is "a Pullman-car porter or something" (397); when "a great rumor went among the crowds" at the fire reporting that "Jimmie Trescott and Henry Johnson had been burned to death, and Dr. Trescott himself had been most savagely hurt"; or when a "man with information" reports that Henry, who was caring for Jimmie, who "had measles or somethin' ... got sleepy or somethin' and upset a lamp, and the doctor he was down in his office" (410). Even what would typically be considered an excellent source of facts—a simple newspaper report—is unreliable when the *Morning Tribune* announces Henry's death.

Imitating the prejudices of adults, children likewise reduce Henry to a hideous monster. During Theresa Page's party, a noise outside immediately scares the children, but as a group they decide to investigate:

> None wished particularly to encounter a dragon in the darkness of the garden, but there could be no faltering when the fair ones in the dining-room were present. Calling to each other in stern voices, they went dragooning over the lawn, attacking the shadows with ferocity, but still with the caution of reasonable beings. They found, however, nothing new to the peace of the night. Of course there was a lad who told a great lie. He described a grim figure, bending low and slinking off along the fence. He gave a number of details, rendering his lie more splendid by a repetition of certain forms which he recalled from romances. For instance, he insisted that he had heard the creature emit a hollow laugh. (428)

The passage dramatizes clearly the strength gained only in a mob mentality. Alone, a person lacks courage "to encounter a dragon," but in a group the same person becomes emboldened "in stern voices" to attack "with ferocity." A group, however, can easily be swayed by someone who misrepresents truth and tells "a great lie." As Marc Antony knew in his famous speech to "Friends, Romans, countrymen" about Brutus in Shakespeare's *Julius Caesar,* a mob is fickle and can easily be swayed. Crane's allusion to "romances" as the source for the "great lie" is his criticism of sentimental fiction so popular during his day that presented life melodramatically rather than realistically. Misrepresenting reality in fiction was, for Crane, morally and aesthetically dishonest, and, as he wrote to a journalist, "[t]o keep close to my honesty is my supreme ambition" (*Correspondence* 196).

Despite the moral blindness of the community, one person, Martha Goodwin, vehemently challenges the portrayal of Henry Johnson as a monster. Her heated conversation with her sister Kate and her neighbor Carrie Dungen is replete with constant references to sight and to rumors as misrepresentations of reality. When Carrie reports the rumor that "Mrs. Howarth heard ... through her front blinds" about the "awful scene between Doctor Trescott and Jake Winter" (*Prose* 442, 441) about Sadie Winter's condition, the image of closed blinds reinforces the inability to see what is there. Despite the widespread belief that Sadie is too sick and terrified to return to school after seeing Henry outside a window at Theresa Page's party, Martha points out the simple fact that she has seen her go to school almost daily. When Carrie defends the town's position, Martha challenges its assumptions. As Carrie says:

> "I don't see how anybody can be blamed for getting angry when their little girl gets almost scared to death and gets sick from it, and all that. Besides, everybody says—"
>
> "Oh, I don't care what everybody says," said Martha.
>
> "Well, you can't go against the whole town," answered Carrie, in sudden sharp defiance.
>
> "No, Martha, you can't go against the whole town," piped Kate, following her leader rapidly.
>
> "'The whole town,'" cried Martha. "I'd like to know what you call 'the whole town.' Do you call these silly people who are scared of Henry Johnson 'the whole town'?"
>
> "Why, Martha," said Carrie, in a reasoning tone, "you talk as if you wouldn't be scared of him!"
>
> "No more would I," retorted Martha.
>
> "O-oh, Martha, how you talk!" said Kate. "Why, the idea! Everybody's afraid of him."
>
> Carrie was grinning. "You've never seen him, have you?" she asked, seductively.
>
> "No," admitted Martha.
>
> "Well, then, how do you know that you wouldn't be scared?"

> Martha confronted her. "Have you ever seen him? No? Well, then, how do you know you would be scared?"
>
> The allied forces broke out in chorus: "But, Martha, everybody says so. Everybody says so." (443)

Although Martha disapproves of Trescott's sheltering Johnson in his home, she is the only person in town who truly empathizes with the doctor's decision to save him. Curiously, when she is first introduced into the story, she is anything but admirable. "[T]he mausoleum of a dead passion" and "probably the most savage critic in town," she knows everyone's business and has "adamantine opinions" about everything (433, 432). Crane, however, structures his story so that readers are put into the same position as the community. At first readers are led to believe that Martha is simply a shrew, but then they discover that, despite her lack of social skills, they have misread her. Given the danger of seeing what is not there—whether on the part of reader or character—it is appropriate that sight be central to "The Monster." Ironically, the person who sees constantly—because his eye will not close—is Henry.

Much has been written about other aspects of the story. As James Hafley argues, it is constructed on the leitmotif of literally and metaphorically losing face. Although Henry literally loses his face, other characters—for example, Alek Williams when he tries to benefit financially from Henry's condition or Bella Farragut when she rejects him after his accident—lose face morally (160). Other critics have analyzed the structure in terms of the 24 chapters of the story. As James Nagel points out, for example, the first 12 chapters show how Henry becomes a monster; the second 12 show how the town becomes monstrous. In both halves the key incident occurs at the middle: Henry gets burned in chapter 6, and Trescott's ostracism begins in chapter 18 ("Significance" 50).

"The Monster" may also have been Crane's response to a cultural and literary interest in the idea of the outcast in the late nineteenth century. According to Alice Hall Petry, the model for Henry Johnson might have been John Merrick, the disfigured Englishman also known as the "Elephant Man," who became famous in 1886 under the care of Dr. Frederick Treves, one of England's most respected doctors. When Merrick died in 1890, his death was widely reported in America. Dr. Treves's treatment of a "monster," however, would continue to be a major topic of discussion in American and English society in the 1890s. A comparison of Merrick and Johnson reveals obvious similarities: both are basically faceless and have only one unblinking eye, both wear a veil to hide their disfigurement, both are taken care of by a caring doctor, and both consider themselves well-mannered gentlemen. The irony, as Petry asserts, is that, whereas Merrick and Treves were respected, Johnson and Trescott are mistreated. Similarly, Crane's story was in all likelihood influenced by Henrik Ibsen's controversial play *An Enemy of the People* (1882). By the early 1890s the play was well known in America. Crane would certainly have known about it, for his two literary mentors, Hamlin Garland and William Dean Howells, had drawn the public's attention to the play in their writings. The similarities between the play and "The Monster" are clear. In the play a respected Dr. Stockmann discovers that the water in the baths that support the local tourist trade is polluted. When he feels morally and professionally obligated to present his findings, the community ostracizes him and his family. Both works contain scenes in which expected guests do not show up and in which representatives of the community, though personally supporting the doctors' decisions, express their inability to do anything because of popular opinion. As Lars Åhnebrink summarized, "[l]ike Ibsen, Crane launched fierce attacks on the mentality of small-town people, their narrowness, their hypocrisy, their complacency, their stupidity, and above all their moral cowardice" (380). Just as Crane responded to the popularity of Ibsen's play, he anticipated the moral smugness and intolerance of small-town America in Sinclair Lewis's influential novel *Main Street* (1920).

WHILOMVILLE STORIES

Although Crane conceded to Harper and Brothers's wish to publish "The Monster," "The Blue Hotel," and "His New Mittens" in book form as *The Monster and Other Stories,* he realized that this was an incongruous mixture of stories. Instead, he envisioned a different collection. Starting in August 1899, he published a series of stories dealing mostly with children in an imaginary town named Whilomville in *Harper's New Monthly Magazine.* They were reprinted posthumously as *Whilomville Stories* in America in August 1900 and England in February 1901. Needing money to pay mounting debts, Crane wrote the stories hastily, and as a result they are uneven in quality. A number of them are based on his own childhood in Port Jervis, where he lived from ages 6 to 11. Read in the order in which they were published serially—the same order used when they were collected as *Whilomville Stories*—they follow "a chronological pattern, moving from summer to summer and including two Christmases to cover a two and one-half year cycle" (Solomon, *From Parody to Realism* 207). Unlike the critical portrayal of complex social issues in "The Monster," these stories depict childhood in small-town America, the one exception being "The Knife," a story about African Americans. Jimmie Trescott, the main character, appears in all but one of the stories. Children go to school, wander the countryside, pretend to be cowboys or pirates, develop crushes, and get in trouble. Children have a secure home life, especially Jimmie, whose parents can afford a cook and a servant.

Though the tone is gently comic and ironic, the world of the children has its own fears, conflicts, and meanness. As a group, the children are often uncivilized. When Homer Phelps does not use the proper pass-word while playing a game of war in "The Trial, Execution, and Burial of Homer Phelps," he is condemned to a mock trial and execution, the price he must pay to be part of Willie Dalzel's gang. Because he chooses at first not to "play it the right way" (*Prose* 1230), he is ostracized and is accepted back into the group only after Jimmie Trescott shows him how to play the game properly. Like Homer, Johnnie Hedge in "The Fight" is another outsider who, after moving to Whilomville, estab-lishes his position in the gang by fighting with, and defeating, Jimmie and Willie Dalzel, the gang leader. The sequel to this story, "The City Urchin and the Chaste Villagers," also deals with power and social rank. In defeating the gang leaders, Johnnie has upset the established order of the children's society so that "the world was extremely anx-ious to know where to place the new-comer" (1249). Willie, however, fights with Johnnie in an attempt to reassert his authority within the gang. The fighting ends only when Johnnie's mother, the "supreme power" (1255), breaks it up.

Though adults function as ultimate figures of authority, at times they find the children's behavior to be amusing. In "Lynx-Hunting," which reintroduces Crane's most famous character, Henry Fleming from *The Red Badge* and "The Veteran," Jimmie Trescott, Willie Dal-zel, and another boy hunt a lynx, even though they do not know what it looks like. The adventure is another example of "their romance of the moment—whether it was of Indians, miners, smugglers, soldiers or outlaws" (1169). After shooting birds, Willie and the other boy give the gun to Jimmie, who is reluctant to fire it but does so because of peer pressure: "if he refused to shoot he would lose his caste, his scalp-lock, his girdle, his honor" (1171). When he aims at a squirrel, however, he accidentally shoots a cow. Frightened by the incident, the boys become more scared when confronted by Fleming and his hired hand about their misbehavior. As Eric Solomon says, "it is the hero of

[*The Red Badge of Courage*], Henry Fleming grown older, who insists that the boys piece through their illusions and accept the responsibility for their actions—the same Henry Fleming who started his battle of life as both a coward and a liar" (212). Rather than punishing the children, however, the two adults "laughed themselves helpless" (1173) when Jimmie tried to convince them that he thought that the cow was actually a lynx. Likewise, in "The Carriage-Lamps," Jimmie gets in trouble when a hired hand, Peter Washington, tells his father that Jimmie has traded with his friend for a pistol. In retaliation against Washington, Jimmie throws stones at him but accidentally breaks lamps in the carriage house. Though Jimmie is confined to his room as punishment, Willie promises to "rescue" him from his "excwable enemies" and "their vile plots" (1215). Meanwhile, Dr. Trescott sneaks into his son's room and listens to the highly imaginative, romantic scheme to rescue Jimmie. Like the Swede in "The Blue Hotel," Jimmie and his friends construct a reality based on dime novels like *The Red Captain: A Tale of the Pirates of the Spanish Main* (1212). Dr. Trescott finds talk about such characters as "the Red Captain," "Hold-up Harry, the Terror of the Sierras," and "a prisoner in yon—in yond—in that there fortress" so amusing that he, like Fleming and his hired hand, laughs so much that he forgets about any further punishment (1214, 1213, 1212).

The stories also capture the excitement and sometimes painful embarrassment of puppy love. In "The Lover and the Tell-Tale," Rose Goldege, the telltale, catches Jimmie writing a love letter to Cora, the girl also in "The Angel-Child" and "The Stove," and promptly announces her discovery to the rest of the children. When the "yelping demoniac mob" baits Jimmie "like little blood-fanged wolves" (1186), a fight breaks out, and he is punished by having to stay after school. As he returns to his seat, he sees "gloating upon him the satanic black eyes of the little Goldege girl" (1188). Jimmie becomes infatuated with another girl and tries to impress her in "Showin' Off," but his attempt runs into a problem when Horace Glenn, the protagonist of "His New Mittens," comes by riding an early version of a bicycle called the velocipede. When the two boys argue about who can ride faster, Horace challenges Jimmie to ride into a ravine but then remembers that he never lets anyone else ride his velocipede. When Horace gets taunted into accepting his own challenge, he gets to the edge of the ravine and accidentally falls in, getting hurt and wrecking his bike. Neither boy ends up showing off to anyone.

Other stories in the collection illustrate additional anxieties that children have growing up. In "Making an Orator," Jimmie Trescott dreads having to speak in front of his class and for two weeks manages to pretend he is sick on each Friday, the day that students must recite a memorized passage. By the third Friday, however, he is forced to attend school. When it is his turn to declaim, he can deliver only a mangled version of Tennyson's "The Charge of the Light Brigade." He is temporarily relieved when the teacher tells him to sit down, with the expectation that he will be better prepared next Friday, but the story ends with the likelihood that Jimmie's anxiety about public speaking will be long lasting. In "Shame," Jimmie is treated like a "social leper" by his peers when he shows up at a picnic with his sandwiches in a lunch pail: the boys "were not competent to care if he had brought his luncheon in a coal bin; but such is the instinct of childish society that they all immediately moved away from him" (1200). And in "A Little Pilgrim" (also published as "A Little Pilgrimage"), Jimmie learns about the hypocrisy of substituting the external trappings of religion for its spiritual core. When the Presbyterian Sunday school he attends suddenly decides to use its money to help victims of a recent earthquake instead of spending it on a Christmas tree, Jimmie is worried he may miss out on Christmas festivities and switches to the Sunday school of the Big Progressive Church, only to discover that this church, not to be outdone by the former, decides also to do without a Christmas tree.

Though Crane's *Whilomville Stories* is not widely known, it captures realistically the joys and traumas of growing up in rural America. It "deserves to be bracketed with Mark Twain's *Adventures of Huckleberry Finn,*" one critic has commented, "as a book ostensibly about boys and actually about mankind. Like *Huckleberry Finn,* Crane's volume of childhood tales has a more mature vision and serious purpose than most American boyhood stories, and it parodies the usual formulae of sentimental, nostalgic, dreamy, and happy childhood tales" (Solomon, *From Parody to Realism* 201). Crane had no desire to write in a popular earlier tradition of stories that unrealistically depicted children as angelic heroes and heroines. As Booth Tarkington—author of *Penrod* (1914), one of America's most popular children's books—wrote, "Crane's children *were* children.... He built them without the waste of a word and at the same time didn't lose a hair of their heads; it's all beautifully, beautifully done" (Wolcott 14).

Works Cited

ABBREVIATIONS

Correspondence: Wertheim, Stanley, and Paul Sorrentino, eds. *The Correspondence of Stephen Crane.* 2 vols. New York: Columbia UP, 1988.

Log: Wertheim, Stanley, and Paul Sorrentino. *The Crane Log: A Documentary Life of Stephen Crane.* New York: G. K. Hall, 1994.

Prose: Crane, Stephen. *Prose and Poetry.* Notes by J. C. Levenson. New York: Library of America, 1984.

Works: Crane, Stephen. *The University of Virginia Edition of the Works of Stephen Crane.* Ed. Fredson Bowers. 10 vols. Charlottesville: UP of Virginia, 1969–76.

REFERENCES

Åhnebrink, Lars. *The Beginnings of Naturalism in American Fiction: A Study of the Works of Hamlin Garland, Stephen Crane, and Frank Norris, with Special Reference to Some European Influences, 1891–1903.* Cambridge: Harvard UP, 1950.

Bacheller, Irving. *Coming Up the Road.* Indianapolis: Bobbs-Merrill, 1928.

Barnes, Robert. "Crane's 'The Bride Comes to Yellow Sky.'" *Explicator* 16 (1958): item 39.

Beer, Thomas. *Stephen Crane: A Study in American Letters.* New York: Knopf, 1923.

Bergon, Frank. Introduction. *The Western Writings of Stephen Crane.* New York: NAL, 1979. 1–27.

Berryman, John. *Stephen Crane*. 1950. Cleveland: World-Meridian, 1962.

———. "Stephen Crane: *The Red Badge of Courage*." *The American Novel from James Fenimore Cooper to William Faulkner*. Ed. Wallace Stegner. New York: Basic Books, 1965. 86–96.

Binder, Henry. "*The Red Badge of Courage* Nobody Knows." *Studies in the Novel* 10 (1978): 9–47.

Blotner, Joseph, ed. *Selected Letters of William Faulkner*. New York: Random House, 1977.

Bowers, Fredson. "Regularization and Normalization in Modern Critical Texts." *Studies in Bibliography* 42 (1989): 79–102.

Brennan, Joseph X. "Ironic and Symbolic Structure in Crane's *Maggie*." *Nineteenth-Century Fiction* 16 (1962): 303–15.

Brooks, Cleanth, R. W. B. Lewis, and Robert Penn Warren, eds. *American Literature: The Makers and the Making*. Vol. 2. New York: St. Martin's, 1973.

[Brooks, Sydney]. "In the School of Battle: The Making of a Soldier." *Saturday Review* [London], 11 Jan. 1896: 44–45. Rpt. in Weatherford 99–103.

Brooks, Sydney. "Mr. Crane and His Critics." *Dial* 20 (16 May 1896): 297–98. Rpt. in Weatherford 146–48.

Brown, Ellen A., and Patricia Hernlund. "The Source for the Title of Stephen Crane's *Whilomville Stories*." *American Literature* 50 (1978): 116–18.

Cady, Edwin H. *Stephen Crane*. Rev. Ed. Boston: G. K. Hall, 1980.

Campbell, Helen. *Women Wage-Earners: Their Past, Their Present, and Their Future*. Boston: Roberts Brothers, 1893.

Carter, Everett. *Howells and the Age of Realism*. Philadelphia: Lippincott, 1954.

Cather, Willa. "When I Knew Stephen Crane." *Stephen Crane: A Collection of Critical Essays*. Ed. Maurice Bassan. Englewood Cliffs, NJ: Prentice-Hall, 1967. 12–17.

Chelifer, [Rupert Hughes]. "Mr. Crane's Crazyquilting." *Criterion* 3 June 1899: 26–27.

Clendenning, John. "Stephen Crane and His Biographers: Beer, Berryman, Schoberlin, and Stallman." *American Literary Realism 1870–1910* 28 no. 1 (1995): 23–57.

———. "Thomas Beer's *Stephen Crane*: The Eye of His Imagination." *Prose Studies* 14 (1991): 68–80.

Colvert, James B. "Crane, Hitchcock, and the Binder Edition of *The Red Badge of Courage*." *Critical Essays on Stephen Crane's* The Red Badge of Courage. Ed. Donald Pizer. Boston: G. K. Hall, 1990. 238–63.

———. Introduction. *Bowery Tales: Maggie and George's Mother*. Vol. 1 of *The University of Virginia Edition of the Works of Stephen Crane*. Ed. Fredson Bowers. Charlottesville: UP of Virginia, 1969. xxxiii–lii.

———. Introduction. *Tales of War*. Vol. 6 of *The University of Virginia Edition of the Works of Stephen Crane*. Ed. Fredson Bowers. Charlottesville: UP of Virginia, 1970. xi–xxxvi.

————. "Stephen Crane: Style as Invention." *Stephen Crane in Transition: Centenary Essays*. Ed. Joseph Katz. DeKalb: Northern Illinois UP, 1972. 127–52.

————. "Stephen Crane's Magic Mountain." *Stephen Crane: A Collection of Critical Essays*. Ed. Maurice Bassan. Englewood Cliffs, NJ: Prentice-Hall, 1967. 95–105.

————. "Structure and Theme in Stephen Crane's Fiction." *Modern Fiction Studies* 5 (1959): 199–208.

Conrad, Joseph. Introduction. *Stephen Crane: A Study in American Letters*. By Thomas Beer. New York: Knopf, 1923. 1–33.

Cook, Robert G. "Stephen Crane's 'The Bride Comes to Yellow Sky.'" *Studies in Short Fiction* 2 (1965): 368–69.

Cosgrove, John O'Hara. Rev. of *Maggie: A Girl of the Streets*. *Wave* 4 July 1896: 14.

Cox, James Trammell. "The Imagery of *The Red Badge of Courage*." *Modern Fiction Studies* 5 (1959): 209–19.

Crane, Jonathan Townley. *Popular Amusements*. New York: Carlton, 1869.

Crane, Stephen. *Prose and Poetry*. Notes by J. C. Levenson. New York: Library of America, 1984.

————. *The Red Badge of Courage: An Episode of the American Civil War*. Ed. Henry Binder. New York: Avon, 1987.

————. *The University of Virginia Edition of the Works of Stephen Crane*. Ed. Fredson Bowers. 10 vols. Charlottesville: UP of Virginia, 1969–76.

Crawford, F. Marion. *The Novel: What It Is*. 1893. Rpt. Westport, CT: Greenwood, 1970.

Crews, Frederick C. Introduction. *The Red Badge of Courage: An Episode of the American Civil War*. New York: Bobbs-Merrill, 1964. vii–xxiii.

Cunliffe, Marcus. "Stephen Crane and the American Background of *Maggie*." *American Quarterly* 7 (1955): 31–44.

Curtin, William M., ed. *The World and the Parish: Willa Cather's Articles and Reviews 1893–1902*. Lincoln: U of Nebraska P, 1970.

Davis, Richard Harding. "Our War Correspondents in Cuba and Puerto Rico." *Harper's New Monthly Magazine* 98 (1898–99): 938–48.

Delbanco, Nicholas. *Group Portrait: Joseph Conrad, Stephen Crane, Ford Madox Ford, Henry James, H. G. Wells*. New York: Carroll & Graf, 1982.

Ellison, Ralph. Introduction. The Red Badge of Courage *and Four Great Stories of Stephen Crane*. New York: Dell, 1960. 7–24.

Emerson, Ralph Waldo. *Emerson's Prose and Poetry*. Ed. Joel Porte and Saundra Morris. New York: Norton, 2001.

Ferrara, Marc, and Gordon Dossett. "A Sheaf of Contemporary American Reviews of Stephen Crane." *Studies in the Novel* 10 (1978): 168–82.

Fried, Michael. *Realism, Writing, Disfiguration: On Thomas Eakins and Stephen Crane*. Chicago: U of Chicago P, 1987.

Garland, Hamlin. "An Ambitious French Novel and a Modest American Story." *Arena* 8 (1893): xi–xii.

———. *Crumbling Idols: Twelve Essays on Art and Literature*. Gainesville, FL: Scholars' Facsimiles & Reprints, 1957.

———. *Roadside Meetings*. New York: Macmillan, 1930.

———. "Stephen Crane: A Soldier of Fortune." *Saturday Evening Post* 28 July 1900: 16–17.

———. "The West in Literature." *Arena* 6 (November 1892): 676.

Greenfield, Stanley B. "The Unmistakable Stephen Crane." *PMLA* 73 (1958): 562–72.

Griffith, Clark. "Stephen Crane and the Ironic Last Word." *Philological Quarterly* 47 (1968): 83–91.

Hafley, James. "'The Monster' and the Art of Stephen Crane." *Accent* 19 (1959): 159–65.

Hart, John F. "*The Red Badge of Courage* as Myth and Symbol." *University of Kansas City Review* 19 (1953): 249–56.

Hawthorne, Nathaniel. *The Complete Novels and Selected Tales of Nathaniel Hawthorne*. Ed. Norman Holmes Pearson. New York: Modern Library, 1937.

Hemingway, Ernest. *Death in the Afternoon*. New York: Scribner's, 1932.

———. *A Farewell to Arms*. 1929. New York: Scribner, 1995.

———. *Green Hills of Africa*. New York: Scribner's, 1935.

———, ed. *Men at War*. New York: Crown, 1942.

Hoffman, Daniel G. "Many Red Devils Upon the Page: The Poetry of Stephen Crane." *Sewanee Review* 102 (1994): 588–603.

———. "Stephen Crane's First Story." *Bulletin of the New York Public Library* 64 (1960): 273.

Howells, William Dean. *The Rise of Silas Lapham*. New York: Signet, 1980.

———. *Selected Literary Criticism, 1898–1920*. Vol. 3 of *A Selected Edition of W. D. Howells*. Ed. Donald Cook et al. 30 vols. Bloomington: Indiana UP, 1993.

Hungerford, Harold R. "'That Was Chancellorsville': The Factual Framework of *The Red Badge of Courage*." *American Literature* 34 (1963): 520–31.

James, Overton P. "The 'Game' in 'The Bride Comes to Yellow Sky.'" *Xavier University Studies* 4 (1965): 3–11.

Johnson, George W. "Stephen Crane's Metaphor of Decorum." *PMLA* 78 (1963): 250–56.

LaFrance, Marston. *A Reading of Stephen Crane*. Oxford: Clarendon, 1971.

LaRocca, Charles J. "Stephen Crane's Inspiration." *American Heritage* 42.3 (1991): 108–09.

Lee, Brian. *American Fiction: 1865–1940*. London: Longman, 1987.

Liebling, A. J. "The Dollars Damned Him." *New Yorker* 5 Aug. 1961: 48–72. Rpt. and abr. in *Stephen Crane: A Collection of Critical Essays*. Ed. Maurice Bassan. Englewood Cliffs, NJ: Prentice-Hall, 1967. 18–26.

Linson, Corwin Knapp. "Little Stories of 'Steve' Crane." *Saturday Evening Post* 11 April 1903: 19–20.

————. *My Stephen Crane*. Ed. Edwin H. Cady. Syracuse: Syracuse UP, 1958.

Lonn, Ella. *Foreigners in the Union Army and Navy*. Baton Rouge: Louisiana State UP, 1951. Reprinted New York: Greenwood, 1969.

Lowell, Amy. Introduction. *The Black Riders and Other Lines*. Vol. 6 of *The Work of Stephen Crane*. Ed. Wilson Follett. New York: Knopf, 1926. ix–xxix.

Marshall, Edward. "Loss of Stephen Crane—A Real Misfortune to All of Us." *New York Herald*. 10 June 1900, sec. 6: 8. Reprinted with minor changes as "Stories of Stephen Crane" in the *San Francisco Call* and in *Literary Life* ns 24 (December 1900): 71–72.

McClurg, Alexander C. "The Red Badge of Hysteria." *Dial* 20 (1896): 227–28. Rpt. in Weatherford 138–41.

McElrath, Joseph. "Stephen Crane in San Francisco: His Reception in *The Wave*." *Stephen Crane Studies* 2 (1993): 2–18.

McFarland, Ronald E. "The Hospitality Code in Crane's 'The Blue Hotel.'" *Studies in Short Fiction* 18 (1981): 447–51.

Mencken, H. L. *The American Language: An Inquiry into the Development of English in the United States*. 3rd ed. New York: Knopf, 1933.

Nagel, James. "The Significance of Stephen Crane's 'The Monster.'" *American Literary Realism* 31 (1999): 48–57.

————. *Stephen Crane and Literary Impressionism*. University Park: Pennsylvania State UP, 1980.

Norris, Frank. *McTeague*. New York: Signet, 2003.

Onderdonk, J.L. Letter defending General Alexander C. McClurg. *Dial* 20 (1896): 263–64. Rpt. in Weatherford 142–43.

Paine, Ralph D. *Roads of Adventure*. Boston: Houghton Mifflin, 1922.

Parker, Hershel. "Getting Used to the 'Original Form' of *The Red Badge of Courage*." *New Essays on* The Red Badge of Courage. Ed. Lee Clark Mitchell. Cambridge: Cambridge UP, 1986. 25–47.

Parker, Hershel, and Brian Higgins. "Maggie's 'Last Night': Authorial Design and Editorial Patching." *Studies in the Novel* 10 (1978): 64–75.

Peck, Harry Thurston. "Some Recent Volumes of Verse." *Bookman* May 1895: 254.

Peck, Jonathan K. *Luther Peck and His Five Sons*. New York: Eaton and Mains, 1897.

Perosa, Sergio. "Naturalism and Impressionism in Stephen Crane's Fiction." *Stephen Crane: A Collection of Critical Essays*. Ed. Maurice Bassan. Englewood Cliffs, NJ: Prentice-Hall, 1967. 80–94.

Petry, Alice Hall. "Stephen Crane's Elephant Man." *Journal of Modern Literature* 10 (1983): 346–52.

Pizer, Donald. "*The Red Badge of Courage* Nobody Knows: A Brief Rejoinder." *Studies in the Novel* 11 (1979): 77–81.

————. "Stephen Crane's *Maggie* and American Naturalism." *Criticism* 7 (1965): 168–75. Reprinted in *Maggie: A Girl of the Streets*. Ed. Thomas A. Gullason. New York: Norton, 1979.

Rahv, Philip. "The Cult of Experience in American Writing." In *Essays on Literature and Politics*. Ed. Arabel J. Porter and Andrew J. Dvoisn. Boston: Houghton Mifflin, 1978. 8–22.

Robertson, Michael. *Stephen Crane, Journalism, and the Making of Modern American Literature*. New York: Columbia UP, 1997.

Sandburg, Carl. *Complete Poems*. Rev. ed. New York: Harcourt, 1970.

———. *Ever the Winds of Chance*. Urbana: U of Illinois P, 1983.

Sanger, William W. *The History of Prostitution: Its Extent, Causes, and Effects throughout the World*. New York: Harper, 1859.

Shulman, Robert. "*The Red Badge of Courage* and Social Values: Crane's Myth of His America." *Canadian Review of American Studies* 12 (1981): 1–19.

Solomon, Eric. *Stephen Crane: From Parody to Realism*. Cambridge: Harvard UP, 1966.

———. "The Structure of *The Red Badge of Courage*." *Modern Fiction Studies* 5 (1959): 220–34.

Sorrentino, Paul. "The Legacy of Thomas Beer in the Study of Stephen Crane and American Literary History." *American Literary Realism 1870–1910* 35 no. 3 (2003): 187–211.

Stallman, R. W. "Crane's Short Stories." *The Houses That James Built and Other Literary Studies*. East Lansing: Michigan State UP, 1961. 103–10.

———. Introduction. *The Red Badge of Courage*. New York: Modern Library, 1951. v–xxxiii.

———. *Stephen Crane: A Biography*. Rev. ed. New York: Braziller, 1973.

———. "Stephen Crane's Revision of *Maggie: A Girl of the Streets*." *American Literature* 26 (1955): 528–36.

Stein, William Bysshe. "Stephen Crane's *Homo Absurdus*." *Bucknell Review* 8 (1959): 168–88.

Turnbull, Andrew, ed. *The Letters of F. Scott Fitzgerald*. New York: Scribner's, 1963.

Twain, Mark. The Gilded Age *and Later Novels*. Ed. Hamlin L. Hill. New York: Library of America, 2000.

Underwood, John Curtis. Rev. of *War Is Kind*. *Bookman* July 1899: 466–67.

Walcutt, Charles Child. *American Literary Naturalism: A Divided Stream*. Minneapolis: U of Minnesota P, 1956.

Weatherford, Richard M., ed. *Stephen Crane: The Critical Heritage*. London: Routledge & Kegan Paul, 1973.

Weiss, Daniel. "The Red Badge of Courage." *Psychoanalytic Review* 52 (1965): 176–96, 460–84.

Wells, H. G. "Stephen Crane: From an English Standpoint." *North American Review* 171 (1900): 233–42. Rpt. in *Stephen Crane's Career: Literary Perspectives and Evaluations*. Ed. Thomas A. Gullason. New York: New York UP, 1972. 126–34.

Wertheim, Stanley, and Paul Sorrentino, eds. *The Correspondence of Stephen Crane*. 2 vols. New York: Columbia UP, 1988.

————. *The Crane Log: A Documentary Life of Stephen Crane*. New York: G. K. Hall, 1994.

————. "Thomas Beer: The Clay Feet of Stephen Crane Biography." *American Literary Realism 1870–1910* 22 no. 3 (1990): 2–16.

Wheeler, Post, and Hallie E. Rives. *Dome of Many-Coloured Glass*. Garden City, NY: Doubleday, 1955.

Wolcott, Alexander. "Stephen Crane's *Whilomville Stories*." *Saturday Review of Literature* 23 Oct. 1937: 14.

Wolford, Chester L. *The Anger of Stephen Crane: Fiction and the Epic Tradition*. Lincoln: U of Nebraska P, 1983.

————. *Stephen Crane: A Study of the Short Fiction*. Boston: Twayne, 1989.

Wyatt, Edith. "Stephen Crane." *New Republic* 11 Sept. 1915: 148–50.

Wyndham, George. "A Remarkable Book." *New Review* [London] 14 (1896): 30–40. Rpt. in Weatherford 106–14.

Bibliography

Note: Though the passages by Crane quoted in this book were published more than 100 years ago and are thus on the public domain, current and readily available sources are cited for the convenience of the reader.

BOOKS

Maggie: A Girl of the Streets, as Johnston Smith. New York: n.p., 1893. Rev. ed., as Stephen Crane. New York: Appleton, 1896; London: Heinemann, 1896.

The Black Riders and Other Lines. Boston: Copeland & Day, 1895; London: Heinemann, 1896.

The Red Badge of Courage. New York: Appleton, 1895; London: Heinemann, 1896.

George's Mother. New York and London: Edward Arnold, 1896.

The Little Regiment. New York: Appleton, 1896; London: Heinemann, 1897.

The Third Violet. New York: Appleton, 1897; London: Heinemann, 1897.

The Open Boat and Other Tales of Adventure. New York: Doubleday & McClure, 1898. English edition: *The Open Boat and Other Stories.* London: Heinemann, 1898.

War Is Kind. New York: Stokes, 1899.

Active Service. New York: Stokes, 1899; London: Heinemann, 1899.

The Monster. New York and London: Harper, 1899. Enlarged ed., London and New York: Harper, 1901.

Whilomville Stories. New York and London: Harper, 1900.

Wounds in the Rain. New York: Stokes, 1900; London: Methuen, 1900.

Great Battles of the World. Philadelphia: Lippincott, 1901; London: Chapman & Hall, 1901.

Last Words. London: Digby, Long, 1902.

The O'Ruddy. By Stephen Crane and Robert Barr. New York: Stokes, 1903; London: Methuen, 1904.

FACSIMILE EDITION

The Red Badge of Courage: A Facsimile Edition of the Manuscript. Ed. Fredson Bowers. 2 vols. Washington, D.C.: Bruccoli Clark NCR Microcard Editions, 1973.

COLLECTIONS

The Collected Poems of Stephen Crane. Ed. Wilson Follett. New York and London: Knopf, 1930.

The Complete Novels of Stephen Crane. Ed. Thomas A. Gullason. New York: Doubleday, 1967.

The Complete Short Stories and Sketches of Stephen Crane. Ed. Thomas A. Gullason. Garden City, NY: Doubleday, 1963.

The New York City Sketches of Stephen Crane. Ed. R. W. Stallman and E. R. Hagemann. New York: New York UP, 1966.

An Omnibus. Ed. Robert W. Stallman. New York: Knopf, 1952.

The Poems of Stephen Crane. Ed. Joseph Katz. New York: Cooper Square, 1966.

Prose and Poetry. Notes by J. C. Levenson. New York: Library of America, 1984.

Stephen Crane in the West and Mexico. Ed. Joseph Katz. Kent, OH: Kent State UP, 1970.

The Sullivan County Sketches of Stephen Crane. Ed. Melvin Schoberlin. Syracuse: Syracuse UP, 1949.

Sullivan County Tales and Sketches. Ed. R. W. Stallman. Ames: Iowa State UP, 1968.

Uncollected Writings. Ed. O. W. Fryckstedt. Uppsala, Sweden: Studia Anglistica Upsaliensia, 1963.

The University of Virginia Edition of the Works of Stephen Crane. Ed. Fredson Bowers. 10 vols. Charlottesville: UP of Virginia, 1969–76.

The War Dispatches of Stephen Crane. Ed. R. W. Stallman and E. R. Hagemann. New York: New York UP, 1966.

The Work of Stephen Crane. Ed. Wilson Follett. 12 vols. New York: Knopf, 1925–27.

BIOGRAPHIES

Benfey, Christopher. *The Double Life of Stephen Crane*. New York: Knopf, 1992.

Berryman, John. *Stephen Crane*. 1950. Cleveland: World-Meridian, 1962.

Cazemajou, Jean. *Stephen Crane*. Univ. of Minnesota Pamphlets on Am. Writers. Minneapolis: U of Minnesota P, 1969.

Colvert, James B. *Stephen Crane*. San Diego: Harcourt, 1984.

Crane, Robert Kellogg. "Stephen Crane's Family Heritage." *Stephen Crane Studies* 4.1 (1995). Issue devoted to the family heritage.

Davis, Linda H. *Badge of Courage: The Life of Stephen Crane*. Boston: Houghton Mifflin, 1998.

Gilkes, Lillian. *Cora Crane: A Biography of Mrs. Stephen Crane*. Bloomington: Indiana UP, 1960.

Linson, Corwin Knapp. *My Stephen Crane*. Ed. Edwin Cady. Syracuse: Syracuse UP, 1958. Memoir about Crane's New York City years.

Raymond, Thomas J. *Stephen Crane*. Newark, NJ: Carteret Book Club, 1923. General essay on Crane.

Robertson, Michael. *Stephen Crane at Lafayette*. Easton, PA: Friends of the Skillman Library of Lafayette College, 1990. Essay on Crane's semester at Lafayette.

Stallman, R. W. *Stephen Crane: A Biography*. Rev. ed. New York: Braziller, 1973.

Surfrin, Mark. *Stephen Crane*. New York: Atheneum, 1992.

FICTIONALIZED BIOGRAPHIES

Beer, Thomas. *Stephen Crane: A Study in American Letters*. New York: Knopf, 1923.

Though this biography is the source of many details about Crane, Beer fabricated most of the letters supposedly from Crane and other writers and invented many of the incidents in the book. For decades, scholars were unaware of this fact. To understand the damage that Beer has done to the study of the life and work of Crane, see the following:

Clendenning, John. "Stephen Crane and His Biographers: Beer, Berryman, Schoberlin, and Stallman." *American Literary Realism 1870–1910* 28 no. 1 (1995): 23–57.

———. "Thomas Beer's *Stephen Crane*: The Eye of His Imagination." *Prose Studies* 14 (1991): 68–80.

Sorrentino, Paul. "The Legacy of Thomas Beer in the Study of Stephen Crane and American Literary History." *American Literary Realism 1870–1910* 35 no. 3 (2003): 187–211.

Wertheim, Stanley, and Paul Sorrentino. "Thomas Beer: The Clay Feet of Stephen Crane Biography." *American Literary Realism 1870–1910* 22 no. 3 (1990): 2–16.

Franchere, Ruth. *Stephen Crane: The Story of an American Writer*. New York: Crowell, 1961. Intended for younger readers.

Zara, Louis. *Dark Rider: A Novel Based on the Life of Stephen Crane*. Cleveland: World, 1961.

LETTERS

Cady, Edwin H., and Lester G. Wells, eds. *Stephen Crane's Love Letters to Nellie Crouse*. Syracuse: Syracuse UP, 1954.

Stallman, R. W., and Lillian Gilkes, eds. *Stephen Crane: Letters*. New York: New York UP, 1960.

Wertheim, Stanley, and Paul Sorrentino, eds. *The Correspondence of Stephen Crane*. 2 vols. New York: Columbia UP, 1988.

NOTEBOOK

The Notebook of Stephen Crane. Ed. Donald and Ellen Greiner. Charlottesville, VA: A John Cook Wyllie Memorial Publication, 1969.

LOG

Wertheim, Stanley, and Paul Sorrentino. *The Crane Log: A Documentary Life of Stephen Crane*. New York: G. K. Hall, 1994.

ENCYCLOPEDIA

Wertheim, Stanley. *A Stephen Crane Encyclopedia*. Westport, CT: Greenwood, 1997.

CONCORDANCES

Baron, Herman. *A Concordance to the Poems of Stephen Crane*. Ed. Joseph Katz. Boston: G. K. Hall, 1974.

Crossland, Andrew T., comp. *A Concordance to the Complete Poetry of Stephen Crane*. Detroit: Gale Research/Bruccoli Clark, 1975.

BIBLIOGRAPHY

Dooley, Patrick. *Stephen Crane: An Annotated Bibliography of Secondary Scholarship*. New York: G, K. Hall, 1992.

Stallman, R. W. *Stephen Crane: A Critical Bibliography*. Ames: Iowa State UP, 1972.

Williams, Ames, and Vincent Starrett. *Stephen Crane: A Bibliography*. Glendale, CA: John Valentine, 1948.

JOURNAL

Stephen Crane Studies. Biannual publication of the Stephen Crane Society, 1992–. Contains articles, reviews, bibliographies, and news about Crane's life and works.

WEBSITE OF THE STEPHEN CRANE SOCIETY

http://www.wsu.edu/~campbelld/crane/index.html. Membership information available at the Web site.

PAPERS

Most of Crane's letters and manuscripts are in the Rare Book and Manuscript Library, Columbia University; Special Collections Research Center, Syracuse University Library; Clifton Waller Barrett Library, University of Virginia Library; the Berg Collection of English and American Literature, New York Public Library; and the Dartmouth College Library.

CRITICAL STUDIES OF STEPHEN CRANE

Åhnebrink, Lars. *The Beginnings of Naturalism in American Fiction: A Study of the Works of Hamlin Garland, Stephen Crane, and Frank Norris, with Special Reference to Some European Influences, 1891–1903.* Cambridge: Harvard UP, 1950.

Bassan, Maurice, ed. *Stephen Crane: A Collection of Critical Essays.* Englewood Cliffs, NJ: Prentice-Hall, 1967.

Bauer, W. John, ed. *William Carlos Williams, Stephen Crane, Philip Freneau: Papers and Poems Celebrating New Jersey's Literary Heritage.* Trenton: New Jersey Historical Commission, 1989.

Bergon, Frank. *Stephen Crane's Artistry.* New York: Columbia UP, 1975.

Bloom, Harold, ed. *Stephen Crane: Modern Critical Views.* New York: Chelsea House, 1987.

———, ed. *Stephen Crane's* The Red Badge of Courage: *Modern Critical Views.* New York: Chelsea House, 1987.

Brown, Bill. *The Material Unconscious: American Amusement, Stephen Crane, and the Economies of Play.* Cambridge: Harvard UP, 1996.

Cady, Edwin H. *Stephen Crane.* Rev. ed. Boston: G. K. Hall, 1980.

Cazemajou, Jean. *Stephen Crane (1871–1900): Écrivain Journaliste.* Paris: Librairie Didier, 1969.

Delbanco, Nicholas. *Group Portrait: Joseph Conrad, Stephen Crane, Ford Madox Ford, Henry James, H. G. Wells.* New York: Carroll & Graf, 1982.

Dooley, Patrick K. *The Pluralistic Philosophy of Stephen Crane.* Urbana: U of Illinois P, 1992.

Fried, Michael. *Realism, Writing, Disfiguration: On Thomas Eakins and Stephen Crane.* Chicago: U of Chicago P, 1987.

Gandal, Keith. *The Virtues of the Vicious: Jacob Riis, Stephen Crane, and the Spectacle of the Slum.* New York: Oxford UP, 1997.

Giamo, Benedict. *On the Bowery: Confronting Homelessness in American Society.* Iowa City: U of Iowa P, 1989. Partly devoted to an analysis of Crane's New York City novels and sketches.

Gibson, Donald B. *The Fiction of Stephen Crane*. Carbondale: Southern Illinois UP, 1968.

———. The Red Badge of Courage: *Redefining the Hero*. Boston: Twayne, 1988.

Gullason, Thomas A. *Stephen Crane's Career: Perspectives and Evaluations*. New York: New York UP, 1972.

———, ed. *Stephen Crane's Literary Family: A Garland of Writings*. Syracuse: Syracuse UP, 2002.

Halliburton, David. *The Color of the Sky: A Study of Stephen Crane*. New York: Cambridge UP, 1989.

Hoffman, Daniel. *The Poetry of Stephen Crane*. New York: Columbia UP, 1957.

Holton, Milne. *Cylinder of Vision: The Fiction and Journalistic Writing of Stephen Crane*. Baton Rouge: Louisiana State UP, 1972.

Johnson, Claudia, ed. *Understanding* The Red Badge of Courage: *A Student's Casebook to Issues, Sources, and Historical Documents*. Westport, CT: Greenwood, 1998.

Katz, Joseph, ed. *Stephen Crane in Transition: Centenary Essays*. Dekalb: Northern Illinois UP, 1972.

Knapp, Bettina. *Stephen Crane*. New York: Ungar, 1987.

LaFrance, Marston. *A Reading of Stephen Crane*. Oxford: Clarendon, 1971.

Mariani, Giorgio. *Spectacular Narratives: Representations of Class and War in Stephen Crane and the American 1890s*. New York: Lang, 1992.

Meredith, James H., ed. *Stephen Crane in War and Peace*. Colorado Springs: United States Air Force Academy, 1999. Special edition of *War, Literature & the Arts: An International Journal of the Humanities*.

Milne, Gordon. *Stephen Crane at Brede: An Anglo-American Literary Circle of the 1890's*. Washington, DC: UP of America, 1980.

Mitchell, Lee Clark. *New Essays on* The Red Badge of Courage. New York: Cambridge UP, 1986.

Monteiro, George. *Stephen Crane's Blue Badge of Courage*. Baton Rouge: Louisiana State UP, 2000.

Nagel, James. *Stephen Crane and Literary Impressionism*. University Park: Pennsylvania State UP, 1980.

Pizer, Donald. *Critical Essays on Stephen Crane's* The Red Badge of Courage. Boston: G. K. Hall, 1990.

Robertson, Michael. *Stephen Crane, Journalism, and the Making of Modern American Literature*. New York: Columbia UP, 1997.

Schaefer, Michael W. *A Reader's Guide to the Short Stories of Stephen Crane*. New York: G. K. Hall, 1996.

Slotkin, Alan Robert. *The Language of Stephen Crane's Bowery Tales: Developing Mastery of Character Diction*. New York: Garland, 1993.

Solomon, Eric. *Stephen Crane: From Parody to Realism*. Cambridge: Harvard UP, 1966.

———. *Stephen Crane in England: A Portrait of the Artist*. Columbus: Ohio State UP, 1964.

Weatherford, Richard M., ed. *Stephen Crane: The Critical Heritage*. London: Routledge & Kegan Paul, 1973.

Wertheim, Stanley, ed. *Studies in* Maggie *and* George's Mother. Columbus, OH: Merrill, 1970.

Wolford, Chester L. *The Anger of Stephen Crane: Fiction and the Epic Tradition*. Lincoln: U of Nebraska P, 1983.

———. *Stephen Crane: A Study of the Short Fiction*. Boston: Twayne, 1989.

Index

About the Author

PAUL M. SORRENTINO is the founder of the Stephen Crane Society and its journal, *Stephen Crane Studies*. Paul is also the co-editor of the *Correspondence of Stephen Crane* and co-author of *The Crane Log: A Documentary Life of Stephen Crane 1871–1900*. Recipient of numerous teaching awards, he is a professor of English at Virginia Tech.